The National Curriculum

Edited by Denis Lawton and Clyde Chitty

Contributors:
Richard Aldrich, Clyde Chitty, Caroline Gipps,
Janet Harland, Denis Lawton, Janet Maw,
Helen Simons, Klaus Wedell, and John White

Bedford Way Papers 33
INSTITUTE OF EDUCATION
University of London

First published in 1988 by the Institute of Education, University of London,
20 Bedford Way, London WC1H 0AL.

Distributed by Turnaround Distribution Ltd., 27 Horsell Road,
London N5 1XL (telephone: 01-609 7836).

The opinions expressed in these papers are those of the authors and do not necessarily
reflect those of the publisher.

British Library Cataloguing in Publication Data

The National Curriculum. — (Bedford Way Papers, ISSN 0261—0078; 33).
  1. Great Britain. Schools. Curriculum
  I. Lawton, Denis, *1931*- II. Chitty, Clyde, III. Series
  375'.00941

  ISBN   0-85473-294-2

Printed in Great Britain by Billing and Sons Ltd., Worcester and London

Typeset by Joan Rose, Institute of Education, University of London

200-204/11-001-122-0288

The National Curriculum

Bedford Way Papers

ISSN 0261—0078

Contents

Preface

For nearly half a century, the educational system of England and Wales has been governed largely by the principles and assumptions of the Education Act of 1944. This in itself is a remarkable achievement. None of the previous major education acts — those of 1870, 1902 and 1918 spring immediately to mind — could claim such longevity. Yet the Act is also remarkable for its omissions. The word 'curriculum' does not appear and there 'is no statutory requirement for the inclusion of any subject in the school timetable, except that of religious education' (Aldrich and Leighton, 1985, p.55).

Now all this is to change. As part of the Education Reform Bill currently before Parliament, the Government is to introduce a national curriculum for the majority of pupils aged five to sixteen. The major significance of this measure and the profound influence it is likely to have on the work of both primary and secondary schools require that it is subjected to detailed critical scrutiny. In this Bedford Way Paper, nine members of the teaching staff of the Institute of Education, University of London, take up that necessary task.

As always, we should like to record our sincere gratitude to Denis Baylis for all his help and support with preparation of the book.

D.L.   C.C.
March 1988

Reference

Aldrich, R. and Leighton, P. (1985), *Education: time for a new Act?* London: Bedford Way Papers 23, Institute of Education, University of London.

Notes on Contributors

Richard Aldrich is senior lecturer in the History of Education at the Institute of Education, University of London. He has taught at school and college of education levels and as a visiting professor in Canada. His publications include *Sir John Pakington and National Education* (1979); *An Introduction to the History of Education* (1982); and (with Patricia Leighton), *Education: time for a new Act?* (1985).

Clyde Chitty (joint editor) has spent twenty years teaching in comprehensive schools in London and Leicestershire. He is now lecturer in the Department of Curriculum Studies at the Institute of Education, University of London. Recent publications include: *TVEI: a perspective* (1985); *Secondary School Examinations* (with Jo and Peter Mortimore) (1986); *Redefining the Comprehensive Experience* (editor) (1987); and *Aspects of Vocationalism* (editor) (1987). Forthcoming publications include: *Access and Achievement at Sixteen-Plus* and *Towards a New Education System: the victory of the New Right?*

Caroline Gipps is lecturer in the Department of Curriculum Studies at the Institute of Education, University of London. She has been involved in research into the impact of LEA testing programmes, the work of the Assessment of Performance Unit, and the role of testing in the GCSE. She is editor of *The GCSE: an uncommon examination* (1986). She started her career as a primary school teacher and has been involved in test development.

Janet Harland is lecturer in the Department of Curriculum Studies at the Institute of Education, University of London. Her main interest is curriculum policy making and its implementation, with particular reference to the 14-18 age group. She has been a TVEI local evaluator since 1984. She is currently preoccupied with how the role of the teacher is affected by MSC programmes, GRIST and the Education Reform Bill.

Denis Lawton (joint editor) is director of the Institute of Education, University of London, where he was previously professor of curriculum studies. He has made a particular study of the control of the school curriculum. His previous publications include *The Politics of the School Curriculum* (1980); *Curriculum Studies and Educational Planning* (1983); and (with Peter Gordon) *HMI* (1987).

Janet Maw is lecturer in the Department of Curriculum Studies at the Institute of Education, University of London. She came to the Institute after working in secondary schools in Birmingham and the Inner London Education Authority. She teaches mainly on courses for headteachers and other senior professionals in schools and LEAs and has published papers on professional development and the management of change, curriculum policy analysis, and curriculum materials.

Helen Simons is chairperson and senior lecturer in the Department of Curriculum Studies at the Institute of Education, University of London. For the past twenty years she has specialized in curriculum and educational evaluation, and has published widely in the fields of school, policy and programme evaluation and the politics of curriculum change. Her current research interests include the impact of government policies on the curriculum and the professionalism of teachers, and local education authorities' response to the management of evaluation and change. Her latest book, *Getting to Know Schools in a Democracy,* was published in 1987.

Klaus Wedell is professor of educational psychology (children with special educational needs) at the Institute of Education, University of London. One of his concerns has been the study of the 1981 Education Act and its implementation through a sequence of DES funded research projects. He has been convenor of a group of special educators who have responded to the national curriculum consultation document, and have prepared a briefing paper on the Education Reform Bill for the Parliamentary Standing Committee.

John White is reader in education at the Institute of Education, University of London, and teaches in the Department of Philosophy of Education. He is author of *Towards a Compulsory Curriculum* (1973); and *The Aims of Education Restated* (1982). He is at present engaged in a book on the personal and social aims of education.

Abbreviations Used

CPG	Curriculum Publications Group
CPVE	Certificate of Pre-Vocational Education
CTC	City Technology Colleges
DES	Department of Education and Science
DoE	Department of Employment
FEU	Further Education Unit
GCE	General Certificate of Education
GCSE	General Certificate of Secondary Education
GRIST	Grant Related In-Service Training
HMI	Her Majesty's Inspectorate
IEA	Institute of Economic Affairs
ILEA	Inner London Education Authority
LAPP	Lower Attaining Pupils Programme
LATE	London Association for the Teaching of English
LEA	Local Education Authority
MSC	Manpower Services Commission
NARTAR	National Association for Race Relations Teaching and Action Research
NATE	National Association for the Teaching of English
NFER	National Foundation for Educational Research
SCDC	School Curriculum Development Committee
SEC	Secondary Examinations Council
TGAT	Task Group on Assessment and Testing
TVEI	Technical and Vocational Education Initiative

Introduction

Denis Lawton and Clyde Chitty

Interviewed by Matthew Parris on ITV's *Weekend World* programme at the beginning of December 1986, the Education Secretary, Kenneth Baker, announced that a third Thatcher administration would introduce a major education bill legislating for a 'national core curriculum' with set objectives. Benchmarks would be established in a wide range of subjects at the ages of nine, eleven and fourteen (later modified to seven, eleven, fourteen and sixteen). Although there was no intention to 'chill and destroy the inventiveness of teachers', Mr. Baker made it clear that 'there would have to be more direction from the Centre as far as the curriculum was concerned'. The proposed 'national curriculum' should be seen as part of the move towards central control in the interests of the pupils. In Mr. Baker's view the comprehensive system was 'seriously flawed'. Only a national curriculum, centrally imposed, could ensure an all-round improvement in standards, particularly at the secondary level.

The Education Secretary went on to expand his thesis in a speech delivered to the North of England Conference on Education at the beginning of January 1987. He described the English education system as 'a bit of a muddle, one of those institutionalized muddles that the English have made peculiarly their own'. It could, moreover, be compared unfavourably with that operating elsewhere in Europe:

> In England we are eccentric in education as in many other things. For at least a century our education system has been quite different from that adopted by most of our European neighbours. They have tended to centralize and to standardize. We have gone for diffusion and variety. In particular, the functions of the State have largely been devolved to elected local bodies; and the school curriculum has largely been left to individual schools and teachers (DES, 1987a).

All this must change as part of a campaign to achieve higher standards. We must both preserve the good features of our present arrangements *and* 'do away with the bad ones' by 'establishing a national curriculum which works through national criteria for each subject area of the curriculum' (ibid.). A sense of urgency was conveyed by the Education Secretary in a second speech in January 1987, this time to the Society of Education Officers' Conference. Here Mr. Baker made it clear that he would not be diverted from his chosen path by the views of 'professional educators':

> . . . I believe that, at least as far as England is concerned, we should now move quickly to a national curriculum . . . I realize that the changes I envisage are radical and far-reaching and may, therefore, be unwelcome to those who value what is traditional and familiar and has often served well in the past. But I believe profoundly that professional educators will do a disservice to the cause of education, and to the nation, if they entrench themselves in a defence of the *status quo*. More and more people are coming to feel that our school curriculum is not as good as it could be and needs to be, and that we need to move nearer to the kind of arrangements which other European countries operate with success, but without sacrificing those features of our own traditional approach which continue to prove their worth (DES, 1987b).

In a further statement at the beginning of April 1987, Mr. Baker announced that two working groups, on mathematics and science, would be set up to advise on attainment targets for children of different ages and abilities and on programmes of study to enable children to reach those targets. They would be the first of a number of working groups with similar tasks. The Government wanted to ensure that pupils received 'a well-balanced foundation curriculum', including not only mathematics and English but also science, foreign languages, history, geography and technology. At the same time, 'clear and challenging attainment targets were needed for the key ages of seven, eleven and fourteen'. Once these were established, it would be possible to 'define the essential content, skills and processes to be taught in each subject' (DES, 1987c).

The proposal to establish 'a national core curriculum' duly became the first of four major reforms outlined in *The Next Moves Forward*, the 1987 Conservative Party Election Manifesto published in May:

It is vital to ensure that all pupils between the ages of five to sixteen study a basic range of subjects — including maths, English and science. In each of these basic subjects, syllabuses will be published and attainment levels set so that the progress of pupils can be assessed at around ages seven, eleven and fourteen, and in preparation for the GCSE at sixteen. Parents, teachers and pupils will then know how well each child is doing. We will consult widely among those concerned in establishing the curriculum (Conservative Party, 1987, p.18).

The National Curriculum consultation document, published two months later (DES, 1987d), listed ten foundation subjects to be taken by all pupils during their compulsory education: English, maths, science, a modern foreign language (except in primary schools), technology, history, geography, art, music and physical education. Of these, English, maths and science would form the 'core' of the curriculum, and the majority of curriculum time at primary level would be devoted to these three subjects. Secondary schools would be expected to devote 30 to 40 per cent of their time to the three core subjects and, in years four and five, 80 to 90 per cent of their time to the foundation subjects. Themes such as health education and information technology would have to be taught through foundation subjects.

Attainment targets would be set for the three core subjects for seven, eleven, fourteen and sixteen-year-olds. They might also be set for other foundation subjects, but for art, music and physical education, there would be 'guidelines' rather than specific attainment targets. National tests, administered and marked by teachers, but moderated by the GCSE examination boards, would measure pupils' progress against the attainment targets at seven, eleven, fourteen and sixteen. Records of achievement would be introduced nationally by 1990.

The consultation document was greeted with a chorus of disapproval and disbelief from educationists, teachers and union leaders alike. Many commentators have pointed out, and we have argued elsewhere (Lawton, 1987; Lawton and Chitty, 1987), that the Government's thinking is 'fundamentally flawed' for a number of reasons.

In the first place, the curriculum is conceived of entirely in terms of subjects, with little or no acknowledgement of the debate which has been going on both inside and outside the DES for at least the last ten years. Although largely educated and trained *within* subject disciplines, teachers have to learn to apply their knowledge and skills in ways which stretch far beyond single subjects and inevitably cross subject boundaries. They have to ask, as HMI working groups have done, what are the essential areas of learning and experience to which all children have a right of access. All this is totally ignored in the consultation document. At the same time, important areas of human experience are almost wholly neglected. There is little or no mention throughout the document of moral education, social and personal development, economic and political understanding — all of which have acquired prominence over the last two decades in an attempt to construct a curriculum which is broad, balanced and relevant to the closing years of the twentieth century.

Despite the fine words about wide consultation, the curriculum clauses of the Bill now going through Parliament show little awareness of the criticisms made of the consultation document. Only in one area is there evidence of a change of heart: the Government has been forced to abandon its idea that the core curriculum should take up at least 80-90 per cent of the secondary school timetable. Launching the Education Reform Bill on 20 November 1987, Kenneth Baker said: 'We don't intend to lay down either in this Bill or in secondary legislation a precise percentage of subjects. It was never the original intention. It will be up to schools, heads and local authorities to deliver the national curriculum and bring children up to the level of attainment targets' (reported in *The Guardian,* 21 November 1987).

* * *

In this Bedford Way Paper, prepared as an urgent contribution to the ongoing debate, the national curriculum is subjected to critical examination by nine members of the teaching staff of the Institute of Education.

In the first chapter, Denis Lawton assesses current government proposals in the context of different political ideologies and general attitudes to welfare. He takes as his starting-point George and Wilding's *Ideology and Social Welfare* (1985) which examines the writings of a number of social theorists and emerges with four broad ideological groups: the anti-collectivists, the reluctant collectivists, the Fabian socialists and the Marxists. Lawton adapts this model to take account of ideological positions unique to education and comes up with four broad classifications: the privatizers; the minimalists or segregators, the pluralists and the comprehensive planners. Seen in this context, the

Baker proposals represent not a radical step forward but 'a retreat away from the ideals of comprehensive education to a thinly-disguised minimalist position, with a few concessions to pluralist ideology'. The plan for a national curriculum may be 'accompanied by some of the common curriculum rhetoric', but 'does not share its ideals'.

The next three contributions assess the DES curriculum proposals in their historical and political context, those by Clyde Chitty and Janet Maw concentrating on the evolution of policy in the recent past.

Richard Aldrich points to the marked similarity between the 1987 curriculum framework and that laid down in the Secondary Regulations issued by the Board of Education in 1904. 'In essence', he argues, 'the proposed national curriculum, in so far as it is expressed in terms of core and foundation subjects, appears as a re-assertion of the basic grammar-school curriculum devised at the beginning of the twentieth century by such men as Robert Morant and James Headlam. . . This curriculum is now to be extended to primary and comprehensive secondary schools.' In a wide-ranging piece, Aldrich goes on to show that not only the range and pattern of the curriculum but even classroom topics and values are now subject to central control, and points out that there are at least two important respects in which the term 'national' as used in the 1987 document can be called into question: those of geography and social class.

Clyde Chitty and Janet Maw both point out the contradictions *within* present government initiatives. Having examined the DES and HMI models of a national curriculum, Chitty argues that while the 1987 document would appear to be in direct descent from the DES curriculum documents of the late 1970s and early 1980s, there are important respects in which it represents a curious departure from earlier DES pronouncements. Above all, it shows little awareness of the vocational thrust of *Better Schools* published in March 1985. At the same time, while it clearly represents the thinking of the DES bureaucracy, it is the only part of the Government's programme which seems to be in line with the trends and developments of the last ten years. For many of the adherents of so-called New Right ideology, a national curriculum is both illogical and unnecessary since, in their view, the whole state system should be dismantled and handed over to market forces. Schools would then be free to devise a curriculum in line with the wishes of parents and local business interests.

Janet Maw expands upon this analysis and suggests that 'the Education Reform Bill, in its present form, is the outcome of ideological conflict, not *between* politicians, HMI and DES bureaucrats, but ideological conflict *within* the political Right in general and the Conservative Party in particular'. In her view, 'the tensions between control and devolution, nationalization and privatization, uniformity and differentiation are inexplicable without such a concept'. She warns that the worst possible outcome of the present struggle against the Bill would be 'the total defeat of the national curriculum, whilst leaving the other proposals untouched. This would open the door to unfettered privatization, differentiation and selection'.

In her chapter, Caroline Gipps assesses the likely effects of testing at seven and eleven on primary-school teaching. While not unaware of the positive features of the proposed national curriculum — and of its examinations — for primary schools, she nonetheless feels that these will be outweighed by the disadvantages. 'Primary schools under the new arrangements will be a good deal more like secondary schools in being under the influence of exam board constraints.' They will have to come to terms with the artefacts of public exams already familiar in the secondary sector: 'more ability banding, more competition, formal teaching relationships and methods, stricter subject boundaries'. Is this, she asks, what we really want for primary education in this country?

Since Caroline Gipps wrote her chapter, the Task Group on Assessment and Training (TGAT) has produced its eagerly-awaited report (DES, 1987e). This report, produced by Professor Paul Black and his colleagues, would seem to be an attempt to bridge the gap between 'bureaucratic' and 'professional' models of curriculum and assessment. It remains, of course, to be seen whether the problems and dangers of national testing, clearly pointed out in the report, will be recognized as important or ignored. There is no guarantee that the report's admirers will be able to overcome the objections of the Prime Minister. As Helen Simons observes in the following chapter, the Education Secretary's warm endorsement of the Black Report reveals 'a dilemma at the heart of the Government's Reform Bill, as well as confirming Mr. Baker's unstated but increasingly obvious discomfiture with the task Mrs. Thatcher has set him'.

The chief concern of the Simons contribution is to focus on an aspect of the Government's curriculum reforms which has received comparatively little publicity: their effect on the professional role of the teacher and the accompanying loss to our education system of the pedagogical and curriculum developments that have taken place since the early 1960s. Simons argues for an alternative vision of better schooling which comprises decentralized curriculum decision-making, local accountability, institutional change and teacher-generated development: all of these crucially dependent upon 'the energizing force of a concept of fully-fledged teacher professionalism'. Measured against this yardstick, the national curriculum is, in her view, 'a folly of unprecedented proportions'.

In her chapter, Janet Harland examines the idea of 'legitimation crisis' — an idea derived from neo-Marxist theories of the state and most fully developed in a work of Jurgen Habermas (1975) — as a way of explaining developments in educational and curriculum policy-making since the mid-1970s, to which the emergence of a national curriculum would appear as a logical conclusion. Seen in this light, the move towards greater central control of the curriculum might be interpreted as 'little more than a knee-jerk response to crisis'. Governments are forced to justify their very existence in a world in which there is an increasing erosion of public confidence in the state's capacity to fulfil its obligations. 'Put simply,' says Harland, 'the less we believe parliamentary government capable of resolving our educational problems, the more politicians charged with running an increasingly discredited system will seek new ways to demonstrate the legitimacy of their policies. They will find that they need to promise more and hence to control more; but the chances of success may well be slim.

Tackling the specific area of special educational needs, Klaus Wedell reminds us that the Warnock Report (DES, 1978) estimated that around twenty per cent of children might at some time in their schooling have special educational needs. According to the provisions of the 1981 Education Act, the LEA has to maintain a 'Statement' in the case of those children whose needs are such as to require the special educational provision. Yet there is no indication that the Education Reform Bill currently going through Parliament takes account of those eighteen per cent or so of children with special educational needs who are taught in ordinary schools without Statements. The only reference to special educational needs occurs in clause 10 of the Bill which permits the national curriculum to be modified in the case of children with Statements. A similar paragraph (paragraph 40) occurs in the 1987

consultation document (DES, 1987) which suggests that only pupils with
Statements might be exempted from parts of the curriculum. Furthermore, argues Wedell, the opting-out clauses of the Bill not only fail
to ensure consideration of support for pupils with special educational
needs, but they also leave the parents of these children specially
vulnerable with regard to the voting procedures since, by definition,
they will always be in a minority and their voice will seldom be heard.

In a concluding chapter, John White points out that there are few
clues in the consultation document to tell us *why* the Secretaries of State
picked their ten foundation subjects and their three core subjects as
particularly important. Indeed, we look in vain for an intellectually satisfying account of the general aims of education. In White's view: 'if
the Secretaries of State had taken the broader view, had seen that
national curriculum planning must begin with aims and then work outwards into their manifold realizations, they would not have been left
with this intellectually impoverished jumble of disconnected ideas hyperbolized as the "national curriculum" '. It is a view doubtless shared
by all the contributors to this Bedford Way Paper.

References

Conservative Party (1987), *The Next Moves Forward*. London: Conservative
Central Office, May.

Department of Education and Science (1978), *Special Educational Needs* (The
Warnock Report). London: HMSO.

——— (1985), *Better Schools*. London: HMSO, Cmnd. 9469.

——— (1987a), 'Kenneth Baker looks at future of education system'. Press
Release 11/87, 9 January.

——— (1987b), 'Kenneth Baker calls for curriculum for pupils of all abilities'.
Press Release 22/87, 23 January.

——— (1987c), 'Legislation next parliament for a national curriculum'. Press
Release 115/87, 7 April.

——— (1987d), *The National Curriculum 5-16: a consultation document*.
London: DES, July.

Department of Education and Science (1987e), *National Curriculum: Task Group on Assessment and Testing: a report.* London: DES, December.

George, V. and Wilding, P. (1985), *Ideology and Social Welfare.* London: Routledge and Kegan Paul.

Habermas, J. (1975), *Legitimation Crisis.* Boston: Beacon.

Lawton, D. (1987), 'Fundamentally flawed', *The Times Educational Supplement,* 18 September.

Lawton, D. and Chitty, C. (1987), 'Towards a national curriculum', *Forum,* Vol.30, No.1, Autumn, pp.4-6.

Ideologies of Education

Denis Lawton

Many educationists welcome the idea of a national curriculum. One of the problems that opponents of the Education Reform Bill face is the difficulty of saying why they accept the principle of a national curriculum but reject the specific form it has taken in the draft legislation. An important reason for this confusion is that the clothes of the educational Left have been stolen by the political Right. Nearly all the arguments in favour of a national curriculum have been associated with egalitarian campaigns for wider educational opportunities, or expressions of children's rights of access to worthwhile educational experiences. But now we are faced with arguments in favour of a national curriculum which have superficial similarities with those put forward earlier to support the principle of a common, or common culture, curriculum. The ideological basis is very different and it is important to distinguish between varieties of national curricula as a first step towards explaining why the Baker national curriculum is educationally unacceptable.

The nature of the immediate problem

In a speech to the North of England Conference on Education in January 1987, the Secretary of State for Education, Kenneth Baker, described the English educational system as 'eccentric' in that it was less centralized and less standardized than those, for example, of France or Germany. He went on to link this with a claim that existing standards were not high enough. He complained about the lack of agreement concerning the fourteen-to-sixteen age group's curriculum, stressing the confusion in schools over the question of balance, and the failure to work out satisfactory objectives:

These weaknesses do not arise in those West European countries where the schools follow more or less standard national syllabuses. In those countries the school system produces results which overall are at least as satisfactory as those produced here; and the teachers are no less professional than ours. Nor do these countries show any sign of wanting to give up the advantages of national syllabuses. So it would be foolish to reject out of hand the idea of moving much nearer to the kind of curricular structure which obtains elsewhere in Western Europe. For my part, I am sure that we must so move. . . (DES, 1987).

As Clyde Chitty and I have pointed out in the Introduction, these justifications for a national curriculum were repeated throughout 1987, sometimes associated with testing at seven, eleven, fourteen and sixteen, and became part of the 1987 Conservative Party election programme. After the election the consultation document, *The National Curriculum, 5-16,* was published (July 1987) and the proposals have been included in the Education Reform Bill.

Problems about a national curriculum

For the last fifteen years or so I have been advocating a common curriculum and a greater degree of central planning of the whole curriculum. I am not therefore opposed to the idea of a national curriculum, but I think we must stress the *professional* issues involved, as well as the different kinds of curriculum that might emerge from different ideological positions.

Mr. Baker's initiative is an interesting example of an ideological change in education which intensified after the election of the Thatcher Government in 1979. The Government has gradually moved closer to policies advocated by the New Right, and it may now be timely to examine how this change in political ideology is affecting policy in education, particularly the school curriculum. In order to make that link, it will be useful first to establish the relationship between political ideology and general attitudes to welfare. George and Wilding (1985) have made an excellent study of this link in their book, *Ideology and Social Welfare.* Education was not central to their concerns, and in some respect did not fit neatly into their classification. Their analysis is, however, both interesting and relevant to the thesis which I want to develop.

In this context it is important to note that contrasting views on education are not simply differences of opinion, but are connected with fundamental values, beliefs and attitudes — in other words, they are ideological differences. Current Conservative arguments about education also have to be seen in the context of more general discussions about the welfare state.

George and Wilding examined the writings of a number of social theorists, from the political Right to the political Left, and emerged with four broad ideological groups: the anti-collectivists; the reluctant collectivists; the Fabian socialists; and the Marxists.

The anti-collectivists

Anti-collectivism was the dominant ideology of nineteenth-century Britain. But by the end of the Second World War it seemed to have disappeared from serious social discussion and was not revived until the early 1970s. Now, Hayek (1973), Friedman (1962) and such right-wing groups as the Institute of Economic Affairs are very influential.

Freedom, individualism and inequality are the fundamental values of the anti-collectivists. Freedom (or liberty) is the most important — an absolute principle. Liberty is defined as freedom from coercion by the state, and is regarded as a natural right. There is an important link between this conception of freedom and the idea of the free market and of the market economy. The market both requires freedom and preserves it.

A free society will promote the second value — individualism — which is both a theory of society and a set of moral maxims. Individualism sees human beings as irrational, self-centred and fallible, but the collaboration of free individuals enables them to transcend these weaknesses; nevertheless, individual responsibility is very important, and what others may regard as social problems (for example unemployment), anti-collectivisits tend to regard as individual responsibility.

The third value is inequality. The notion of social justice is not accepted; it is 'entirely empty and meaningless' according to Hayek. Furthermore, egalitarianism is incompatible with freedom. Inequality is supported on pragmatic grounds as well as moral; for example, Sir Keith Joseph (1976) suggested that the redistribution of wealth had reached the point where it was discouraging wealth creators, and turning Britain into a totalitarian slum. The most efficient way to run the economy and other aspects of the social system is the free market, or *laissez-faire*. It is superstition, according to Hayek, to think that governments can improve the world.

The reluctant collectivists

Reluctant collectivists lack the anti-collectivists' complete faith in unregulated *laissez-faire,* but still approve strongly of private enterprise and capitalism, believing it to be the best economic system, even if requiring some regulation and reform. Capitalism has faults but they can be corrected. Keynes adopted this kind of pragmatic approach to capitalism in the field of economics, and so did Galbraith; more recently Sir Ian Gilmour (1978) has rejected absolute values and theories on political and social questions as inappropriate for the Conservative Party.

The view of Sir William Beveridge (the war-time architect of the welfare state in Britain) was that freedom is an important value in itself, but also compatible with planning. The evils which freedom brings relief from include government *and* both overbearing poverty and other social problems. At the same time individualism, self-help, private enterprise and the capitalist system itself are highly valued.

Reluctant collectivists approve of inequality for economic, social and cultural reasons, but they tend to be against gross inequalities. They approve of progressive taxation, for example, and of other ways of narrowing the inequality gap. On economic organization, some reluctant collectivists, like David Owen, argue specifically for the mixed economy: neither pure capitalism nor socialism will do. Capitalism is efficient and beneficial in many respects but has four shortcomings:

1. It is not self-regulating (for example, the inability to control inflation);

2. It is wasteful and misallocates resources ('private affluence and public squalor');

3. It does not abolish injustice and poverty (freedom has to be moderated by other values);

4. It creates conditions which can threaten political stability ('misery generates hate').

The general policy is, therefore, not *laissez-faire* but harnessing market forces for the public and private good by means of government planning. Reluctant collectivists still dislike government interference, and give only lukewarm support to state intervention on such matters as incomes policy and welfare. The Conservative Party is still generally in the reluctant collectivist category, but has moved closer towards the anti-collectivist position; the 'wets' have lost out to the hardliners.

Fabian socialists

For Fabians there are three central values — equality, freedom and fellowship (or fraternity) — and two derivative values — democratic participation (derived from equality plus freedom) and humanitarianism (derived from equality plus fellowship). For Tawney (1921) equality was fundamental, 'the necessary corollary of the Christian conception of man'. The case for equality rests on four grounds: social integration, economic efficiency, natural justice and individual self-realization. As well as Tawney, Titmuss, Crosland and Meacher are among those who have written from this ideological position in Britain. There is wide agreement about the need to eliminate economic and social inequality but confusion about the precise meaning of equality. They also disagree among themselves about the relative importance of freedom and equality; but all stress the importance of fellowship. Meacher (1982), for example, contrasts the elitism, materialism and competitiveness of capitalism with the more desirable sharing, altruism and co-operation of socialism. Class conflict, according to this view, is an inevitable feature of capitalism, but Fabians tend to disagree about whether or not capitalism is breaking down or simply changing.

The task of government is to control and modify the capitalist system. For this, government intervention cannot be minimal but must be 'planning for freedom' on a grand scale. But the planners and other officials must always be accountable to the public. Social services are vital, but some Fabians are suspicious that they might be a bribe offered by the capitalist class in return for a compliant workforce. Fabians tend to be on the side of universal provision of social services rather than selectivity (by means testing), but Crosland for example, was not always in favour of universal, free availability. Similarly, Fabian socialists are divided to some extent on the balance between public and private provision. On the whole, they are against private provision in education and health because they tend to increase inequality, but they are not clear on a policy for their abolition.

The Marxists

A major emphasis in Marxist writing is the exploitation and alienation of the working classes. Marxists tend to see individual freedom in broad terms: they want to remove obstacles to human emancipation and self-realization. Liberty and equality are not opposing values but are complementary. Laski (1934), for example, argued that liberty cannot exist in the presence of special privilege, nor where the rights of some depend on the pleasures of others, nor where state action is biased in favour of one group. In other words, liberty cannot exist in a capitalist society.

There are two different, but not incompatible, explanations of welfare services in the Marxist literature: first, they are seen as concessions exacted as a result of hard-won battles fought by the Labour Movement; second, they are interpreted as a deliberate ploy by the capitalist class to avoid revolution and to adapt to the changing needs of capitalism. Marxists usually insist that the abolition of the capitalist system must precede the achievement of freedom, equality and fellowship. Only then will genuine welfare be possible.

Reformulation of political ideologies as applied to education

I find it necessary to depart from the George and Wilding classification of ideologies for several reasons. For example, ideological views on education tend to be more complex than attitudes to welfare generally. There are some similarities but not enough to justify simply taking over the George and Wilding classification. In particular, it would be difficult to identify the 'Marxist' position on education since there are probably four or five different Marxist views on the relationship between education and society, education and culture. Nevertheless, I shall want to draw upon their general thesis as well as some of their specific insights into the link between ideology and social policy.

I want to refer to four ideological positions on education: *1.* the privatizers; *2.* the minimalists or segregators; *3.* the pluralists; *4.* the comprehensive planners.

The privatizers

There has recently been a renewal of interest in the view that education is essentially a private concern rather than something appropriate for government responsibility. The 'pure' version of this view recommends privatizing all education, from pre-school provision to university. Local education authorities would be disbanded, all schools would be run by boards of governors or by private companies. Parents would have complete freedom to choose — moderated only by their ability to pay.

The ideological background for this view is *laissez-faire* capitalism with total reliance on market mechanisms to control the relation between supply and demand in education. 'Choice' is the key concept. If there are some who doubt whether privatizers, in a pure form, still exist, they should note the following:

> The blind, unplanned, uncoordinated wisdom of the market . . . is overwhelmingly superior to the well-researched, rational, systematic, well meaning, co-operative, science-based, forward-looking, statistically respectable plans of governments . . . The market system is the greatest generator of national wealth known to mankind: co-ordinating and fulfilling the diverse needs of countless individuals in a way which no human mind or minds could ever comprehend, without coercion, without direction, without bureaucratic interference (Joseph, 1976).

Sir Keith Joseph was at heart a privatizer, but when he became Secretary of State for Education in 1981, he was persuaded by his civil servants to adopt a more politically acceptable stance. A difficulty about this category is that it is not easy to find examples in a 'pure' form; privatizers tend to 'water down' their public utterances. Nevertheless, the ideology is very important as a strand of Conservative thinking on education and as an influence on policy. As recently as 6 August 1987, Sir Alfred Sherman, who has been an adviser to the Conservative Party, wrote in *The Daily Telegraph* advocating the privatization of all schools. His is by no means a lone voice.

Privatizers would not be in favour of a national curriculum. They favour as much diversity as possible both *between* schools and *within* schools. Choice is all important. It is the function of the school to provide a curriculum which offers choice according to aptitude, future educational aspirations and occupation. The curriculum must cater for as much choice as possible; the teacher's task is to guide students through choices to make sure that foolish or unsuitable options are avoided. Classic examples of this kind of curriculum pattern may be seen in well known Public (that is, private) Schools in Britain.

The minimalists

Minimalists believe in a mixed economy in education. The state should pay for basic provision (as cheaply as possible) and parents would have the right and privilege of buying additional extras or of opting out of the state system altogether. This led to what Tawney (1921) criticized as a system run by those who felt that it was not good enough for their own children. Some voucher systems could operate within this scenario, for example that advocated by Stuart Sexton (1987). The Assisted Places Scheme is also characteristic of the thinking behind minimalism, by signalling clearly that state schools are not really good enough for bright children. Mr. Baker's city technology colleges represent another example of this approach.

Minimalists also tend to be segregators; they want to separate children according to social class, or supposed intellectual ability, perhaps also by sex. Minimalists are not in favour of a common curriculum, but they may advocate a low-level basic national curriculum enforced by tests. Accountability and value for money are the key concepts.

The pluralists

Pluralists want to provide a state system so good that there would be little or no incentive to use independent schools. Their regard for individual freedom of choice would not, however, allow them to legislate private schools out of existence. Freedom to choose is more important than social justice or equality of opportunity. Fabian socialists such as Tony Crosland somewhat reluctantly came to this point of view. The pragmatists in the group would argue that it would be impossible, even if desirable, to prevent parents sending their children to independent schools, because it is alleged that some independent schools already have contingency plans to move to Ireland or elsewhere if they were threatened by punitive or preventative legislation.

Pluralists invented such terms as 'parity of esteem' for the different but equal types of secondary school within the tripartite system. They tend to hold meritocratic beliefs in education, favouring the metaphor of 'the ladder of opportunity' rather than that of 'the broad highway'.

They favour selection by choice — pupil self-selection — rather than imposed limitations of access. Some pluralists are uneasy about the idea of a common curriculum, because they doubt the capacity of those of 'lower ability' to follow a worthwhile common curriculum. This kind of thinking has led some comprehensive schools into the trap of the now discredited 'core plus options' curriculum. Some Tory politicians might be included in this catgegory — Butler and Boyle, and possibly since his speech in December 1987, Ted Heath.

The comprehensive planners

'Comprehensive planners' is a useful term for those who recognize the need to change the secondary curriculum to adjust to the needs of mass education. Comprehensive planners argue that a watered-down version of pseudo high-culture curricula will not do for a society committed to genuine secondary education for all. They also tend to criticize the grammar-school curriculum for other reasons — epistemological, cultural and social as well as political (Lawton, 1983). Attempts to devise a common curriculum rest on ideological assumptions about common culture and common schools without denying individual differences and the need to provide for individual opportunities within a common plan. 'Common culture' is the key concept.

The late Raymond Williams (1961) talked of a common curriculum in the context of his account of the history of education in the United Kingdom. In 1973 I attempted to outline a strategy for planning a 'common culture individualized curriculum' that would avoid uniformity (Lawton, 1973). Comprehensive planners will generally tend to be in favour of centralized planning: Halsey (1983), for example, put forward a proposal involving the possibility of LEAs being abolished. But they will also be concerned with the professionalism of teachers.

In practice, many comprehensive schools have found it very difficult to escape completely from the dead hand of the grammar school. The curricula of most comprehensive schools have tended to be less academic versions of the grammar school curriculum. There has also been a tendency to equate less academic with less intelligent, less worthy and less important. But for true comprehensive planners, access must be completely open — the aim is a good general education for all; the metaphor 'the broad highway'. Excellence is defined in terms of enabling individuals to become autonomous learners, successful self-educators across a wide range of cultural experiences.

Ideology and the changing curriculum
Until recently in England, the educational debate was mainly between the minimalists and the pluralists — the middle ground of the moderate left represented by Tony Crosland and moderate Conservatives such as Edward Boyle. At the same time there was some discussion within the Labour Party (and elsewhere) about the desirability of moving towards what I have labelled 'the comprehensive planners' position. But for the last ten years, with the 'end of consensus' stimulated by the emergence of Margaret Thatcher as the Tory Party leader, the debate about education, in common with other social policies, has polarized. There has been a revival of the privatizing ideology, and the debate on the Left about comprehensive planning has sharpened, without, as yet, much sign of ideology being converted into political policy.

In the run-up to the 1987 General Election, education became an important issue. It is interesting that although the record of the Conservative Party on education spending was very poor, they were still able to appear to be the party with radical innovative policies. They achieved this by emphasizing the importance of choice in education. The Labour Party was left in the unfortunate position of merely promising to run the existing system more efficiently and with more resources. The opportunity was missed of exploring the means of allowing greater choice within schools rather than merely opposing the populist policy of choosing between schools. Such a policy would have called for strategies of curriculum planning yet to be incorporated into Labour Party programmes.

Conclusion
Seen in this context, the Baker proposals for a national curriculum represent not a radical step forward but a retreat away from the ideals of comprehensive education to a thinly-disguised minimalist position, with a few concessions to pluralist ideology. Mr. Baker's plan for a national curriculum may be accompanied by some of the common curriculum rhetoric, but does not share its ideals. Like the earlier Conservative proposals for the Assisted Places Scheme (1981), the 1987 education reforms, with their 'opting out' facilities, signal a clear message: 'State schools may be good enough for others, but not for our children.'

References:

Crosland, C.A.R. (1956), *The Future of Socialism*. London: Cape.

Crosland, S. (1982), *Tony Crosland*. London: Cape.

DES (1977), *Curriculum 11-16* (HMI Red Book One). London: HMSO.

Friedman, M. (1962), *Capitalism and Freedom*. Chicago:

George, V. and Wilding, P. (1984), *Ideology and Social Welfare*. London: Routledge and Kegan Paul.

Gilmour, I. (1978), *Inside Right*. London: Quartet.

Halsey, A.H. (1983), 'Schools for democracy', in J. Ahier and M. Flude (eds.), *Contemporary Education Policy*. London: Croom Helm.

Hayek, F.A. (1973), *Law, Legislation and Liberty, Vol.I Rules and Order*. London: Routledge and Kegan Paul.

Hillgate Group (1986), *Whose Schools? A Radical Manifesto*. London: Hillgate Group.

Joseph, Sir Keith (1976), *Stranded on the Middle Ground*. London: Centre for Policy Studies.

Laski, H. (1934), *The State in Theory and Practice*. London: Allen and Unwin.

Lawton, D. (1973), *Social Change, Educational Theory and Curriculum Planning*. Sevenoaks: Hodder and Stoughton.

——— (1983), *Curriculum Studies and Educational Planning*. Sevenoaks: Hodder and Stoughton.

Meacher, M. (1982), *Socialism with a Human Face*. London: Allen and Unwin.

Sexton, S. (1987), *Our Schools: a radical policy*. London: Institute of Economic Affairs.

Sherman, Sir Alfred, (1987), 'How everyone could have a Public School education', *The Daily Telegraph,* 6 August.

Tawney, R.H. (1921), *The Acquisitive Society*. London: Bell and Sons.

Titmuss, R.M. (1968), *Commitment to Welfare*. London: Allen and Unwin.

Williams, R. (1961), *The Long Revolution*. Harmondsworth: Penguin.

The National Curriculum: an historical perspective

Richard Aldrich

This chapter is divided into five parts. The first identifies the immediate and longer-term origins of the concept of a centrally directed national curriculum; the second considers the recent historical record of central authority in education. The next two sections focus upon the implications of the terms 'national' and 'curriculum', as employed both in the current consultation document, and in a wider context. Finally, some brief conclusions are drawn.

I

Historians of education are sometimes accused of engaging in a perpetual search for a better yesterday. Much of this chapter, indeed, is concerned with the past, not however for the purpose of applauding the achievements of our forbears, nor for lamenting the problems of the present. The aim is to identify the fundamental issues, both in terms of problems and of solutions, which have for a century and more surrounded the themes of national education and a national curriculum, and to place the current proposals in their historical context.

Today's debates about a national curriculum have stemmed from many sources, not least, at the time of writing, from the consultation document *The National Curriculum, 5-16,* issued in July 1987 (DES, 1987), and its subsequent incorporation into a major Education Reform Bill. This document embodies two main proposals. The first is that pupils between the ages of five and sixteen in state schools should follow a centrally-directed curriculum comprising core and foundation subjects. The second is that pupils should be tested at ages seven, eleven,

21

fourteen and sixteen. The rationale for such proposals is that some state schools provide their pupils with a curriculum which is inappropriate both to their needs and to those of society at large. Nationwide testing is deemed to be necessary because standards of pupil attainment are low, particularly when compared with those of children in such countries as Japan and West Germany.

To an historian the most striking feature of the proposed national curriculum is that it is at least 83 years old. State secondary schools were established by the 1902 Act and in 1904 the Board of Education issued regulations which prescribed the syllabus for pupils up to the ages of sixteen or seventeen in such schools.

The Course should provide for instruction in the English Language and Literature, at least one language other than English, geography, history, mathematics, science and drawing, with due provision for manual work and physical exercises, and in a girls' school for Housewifery (Gordon and Lawton, 1978, pp.22-3).

A comparison with the curriculum proposed in the 1987 document is instructive.

1904	*1987*
English	English
Mathematics	Mathematics
Science	Science
History	History
Geography	Geography
Foreign Language	Modern Foreign Language
Drawing	Art
Physical Exercise	Physical Education
Manual Work/Housewifery	Technology
	Music

There is such a striking similarity between these two lists that it appears that one was simply copied from the other, although the term 'modern foreign language' in the 1987 list excludes Latin which featured prominently in the secondary school curricula of 1904. Thus, only music of the 1987 list was not a compulsory subject in 1904. The following list of subjects from 1935, however, indicates both the continuing tradition, and an even closer match with the list of 1987.

Except with the previous permission of the board, adequate provision must be made for instruction in the English Language and Literature, at least one language other than English, geography, history, mathematics, science, drawing, singing, manual instruction in the case of boys, domestic subjects in the case of girls, physical exercises and for organized games (Gordon and Lawton, 1978,p.28).

Thus in essence the proposed national curriculum, in so far as it is expressed in terms of core and foundation subjects, appears as a reassertion of the basic grammar school curriculum devised at the beginning of the twentieth century by such men as Robert Morant and James Headlam (Eaglesham, 1967, pp.58-61). This curriculum is now to be extended to primary and comprehensive secondary schools.

There are some grounds, however, for supposing that the consultation document, though entitled *The National Curriculum,* is essentially concerned with testing, and that the list of core and foundation subjects is simply designed to facilitate that testing. In this respect, the historical antecedent is clearly the Revised Code of 1862. In that year Robert Lowe, member of a government which was determined to reduce central expenditure on elementary education, introduced a system of payment by results whereby grants to schools were based upon standards of attainment reached by children in a very limited range of subjects — initially the three Rs. So dominant was this philosophy that children came to be grouped in standards rather than in forms or classes. The curriculum was thus subordinated to the demands of a test procedure which was itself employed to justify a reduction in educational expenditure, although this latter aim was expressed in terms of securing value for money.

In 1985 *Better Schools* indicated a similar set of priorities when it concluded that 'The Government's central aim is to improve standards in schools, using the available resources to yield the best possible return' (DES, 1985, p.90). That improvement in standards was quantified in terms of the Government's 'longer-term aim to raise pupil performance at all levels of ability so as to bring 80-90 per cent of all 16 year old pupils at least to the level of attainment now expected and achieved by pupils of average ability in individual subjects' (DES, 1985, p.26).

The National Curriculum 5-16 (DES, 1987, pp.2-3) shows the Government's impatience in the face of the complexity and magnitude of the task it has undertaken. The whole document represents a hasty and ill-considered departure from the policy of partnership and purposeful progress expressed in *Better Schools.*

II

To state the obvious, there can be no doubt that *The National Curriculum 5-16* and the Education Reform Bill mark the reassumption by central government of the control and direction of the school curriculum, a control which had largely been ceded in elementary schools by the later 1920s and in secondary schools by 1944. The very title of the Board of Education's Handbook of *Suggestions for the Consideration of Teachers and others concerned with the Work of Public Elementary Schools* indicated a major change from the era of payment by results. A prefatory memorandum to the Handbook of 1905 declared that:

> The only uniformity of practice that the Board of Education desire to see in the teaching in Public Elementary Schools is that each teacher shall think for himself, and work out for himself such methods of teaching as may use his powers to the best advantage and be best suited to the particular needs and conditions of the school . . . (Board of Education, 1905, p.6).

This statement was repeated as a prefatory memorandum in subsequent editions, editions which acknowledged that the child, rather than any rigid curriculum or syllabus, was the true starting-point in education. Thus the Handbook of 1929 advised that 'The curriculum must vary to some extent with the qualifications of the teaching staff', and that 'Variations in the curriculum will often correspond to the special needs and circumstances of the scholars' (Board of Education, 1929, pp.38-9). In 1937 it was acknowledged that the elementary school curriculum had 'arisen in a somewhat haphazard way', but teachers were warned that for younger children 'any division of experience into separate time-table subjects is at best an artificial business', and overall that it was not possible 'to lay down any rule as to the exact number of the subjects which should be taken in an individual school' (Board of Education, 1937, pp.36-9).

In 1944 central government stepped back from control of curriculum except in matters of religious worship and education. During the second reading of the Education Bill, James Chuter-Ede, parliamentary secretary of the Board of Education, declared that 'State control of the curriculum prevented the development of a wise and sound system of education . . . there is no one curriculum for every child' (*Hansard,* H of C, Vol.396, Col.497, 20 January 1944). With the advantage of hindsight one might also question the effectiveness of central government control of the curriculum in the one area in which it retained responsibility. Section 25 of the 1944 Act prescribed, and still prescribes, that 'the school day in every county school and in every voluntary school shall begin with a collective act of worship on the part of all pupils'. It further requires that 'religious instruction shall be given in every county school and in every voluntary school'. At the end of 1985, however, a survey carried out by *The Times Educational Supplement* showed that only 6 per cent of secondary schools were complying with the strict requirement for collective worship, although the figure rose to 35 per cent if split sites were treated as separate institutions (*The Times Educational Supplement,* 20 December 1985).

Even in 1985 the Conservative Government still refrained from direct curriculum control. *Better Schools* declared that:

> . . . it would not in the view of the Government be right for the Secretaries of State's policy for the range and pattern of the five to sixteen curriculum to amount to the determination of national syllabuses for that period. It would however be appropriate for the curricular policy of the LEA, on the basis of broadly agreed principles about range and pattern, to be more precise about, for example, the balance between curricular elements and the age and pace at which pupils are introduced to particular subject areas (e.g. a foreign language) . . . The Government does not propose to introduce legislation affecting the powers of the Secretaries of State in relation to the curriculum (DES, 1985, pp.11-12).

Two years later that statement has been repudiated. A revolution, or perhaps a counter-revolution, is about to take place. The Secretary of State, moreover, has already in Section 46 of the Education (No.2) Act, 1986, assumed the power to ensure that sex education shall be given in such a manner as to encourage pupils to have 'due regard to moral considerations and the value of family life'. In September 1987 his directive concerning teaching about homosexuality showed that not only the range and pattern of the curriculum, but even the classroom topics and values are now subject to central control. History is another area in which central government intervention in respect of subject matter and values appears to be imminent. On 23 January 1987 in a speech to education officers, Kenneth Baker declared that history was 'one subject which is causing me growing concern as I learn more about what pupils are actually being taught'.

There is little doubt that since 1945 Britain has experienced periods of relative economic decline, decline which in recent years has been accompanied by widespread unemployment. Attention has been drawn to the low proportion of 16-21 year olds in education in this country and to shortages of skilled workers in such areas as engineering. The present Government points to the failure of some LEAs and schools to provide adequate curricula, and urges the example of economically more successful countries in which centrally-controlled curriculum arrangements exist. *The National Curriculum 5-16* states explicitly that the purpose of a national curriculum is to 'develop the potential of all pupils and equip them for citizenship and for the challenges of employment in tomorrow's world . . . We must raise standards consistently, and at least as quickly as they are rising in competitor countries' (DES, 1987, pp.2-3).

It is extremely difficult indeed to determine whether a more centralized and standardized curriculum of the type proposed would improve this country's economic performance. Perhaps the answer would be to pay teachers more. Teachers in our competitor countries certainly have higher salaries and status than they do here. Another solution might be to address the problem of the quality of management in British industry. The continuing cult of the 'gentleman amateur', the prolongation of the ideals and attitudes of an imperial elite, still nurtured in the Public Schools and in so many areas of British society, are adduced by foreign observers as the main cause of our economic problems (Wiener, 1981). It is interesting to note that many of the successful inner city schools which Mr. Baker visited in the USA in September 1987 are committed to the pursuit of a particular and specialized, as opposed to a general curriculum.

There is considerable evidence indeed that Britain's economic failures, in so far as they may be related to a failure in education, stem not so much from the inability or unwillingness of LEAs and teachers to provide adequate curricula, as from the refusal of central government to fulfil its statutory duty in respect of basic institutional and financial provision. Two examples may be cited. In 1918 the Fisher Education Act provided for the raising of the school-leaving age to 14, for continuation schools for those aged 14-16 not in full-time education, and for the subsequent extension of continuation schooling to 16-18 year olds. Only in Rugby, however, did continuation schooling succeed. Neither central government nor local authority was prepared to do its duty under this Act. During the Second World War as Britain's shortages of skilled workers became apparent and specialized training centres had to be established, the government of the day, in the shape of both Butler and Chuter-Ede, assured Parliament and the country that such a state of affairs would not be allowed to continue in the post-war world. The 1944 Act made detailed provision for the establishment of county colleges for the compulsory part-time education up to the age of 18 of all young people who were not engaged in full-time schooling. That education, which was to have included practical, vocational and physical training, might well have averted many of the economic and social problems currently facing this country. But the county colleges were not established. Once again this failure must be laid firmly at the door of central government. Resources were not provided; as in the case of the 1918 Act local authorities were not required to fulfil their statutory duty and, in circumstances far more reprehensible than those which existed after 1918, this part of the 1944 Act became a dead letter. The most curious, indeed outrageous, proposal contained in *The National Curriculum 5-16* is that which announces that the Education Bill of 1987 will give the Secretaries of State the reserve power '. . . to regulate the qualifications and syllabuses offered to full-time pupils aged 16-19 in schools and colleges' (DES, 1987, p.19).

Thus the recent record of central government in matters of education has not been impressive. The failure to invest sufficient resources is shown by the present dilapidated state of school buildings. The central educational authority in England and Wales has few staff and virtually no experience in owning and running schools or other educational establishments, or in determining curricula and examinations. Advisory bodies, including the councils specifically established under the 1944 Act to advise the Minister of Education, have been destroyed. The present Government regularly rejects the advice of educational experts including its own, or rather Her Majesty's, Inspectors. Typically the proposed National Curriculum Council and School Examinations and

Assessment Council will be appointed by the Secretary of State 'in a personal rather than a representative capacity' (DES, 1987, p.16). The 1944 Act, moreover, was preceded by an extensive period of consultation based upon a genuine desire for partnership. This may be contrasted with the situation in 1987 when Kenneth Baker declared his determination to carry on with his own proposals in spite of any advice and objections afforded by other partners within the educational service, and originally allowed a mere matter of two months for responses to the consultation document, *The National Curriculum 5-16*. The unsatisfactory nature of this situation is compounded by the many contradictions which abound in the Government's own policy. Three examples will suffice. Section 18 of the Education (No.2) Act 1986 regarding the duties of head teachers in respect of the curriculum has already been superseded by the paragraph 58(iv) of *The National Curriculum 5-16*. This document itself, moreover, is internally inconsistent over such matters as the first age of testing (variously described as 'seven', 'around the ages of seven', 'seven (or thereabouts)', 'a different age than seven', and over attainment targets. Such uncertainty is not confined to the curriculum and to testing. In respect of grant maintained schools, which are to be allowed to opt out of LEA control, the Secretary of State for Education and Science clearly believes that these will be relatively few in number; the Prime Minister, on the other hand, intends this to be an educational revolution, comparable to the sale of one million council houses!

III

There are two particular respects in which the term 'national' as used in the document *The National Curriculum 5-16* can be called into question — those of geography and social class. The national curriculum is not to be applied, according to this document, to Scotland or to Northern Ireland. Does a Government which believes so strongly in ensuring that 'all pupils, regardless of sex, ethnic origin and geographical location, have access to broadly the same good and relevant curriculum' (DES, 1987, p.3) intend to apply this to all parts of the United Kingdom? Would this not be an appropriate time to end the anomalous situation whereby responsibility for education at some, but not all levels, falls not to the Secretary of State for Education and Science but to other ministers?

Nor is the national curriculum to be applied to independent schools, although the 'Secretaries of State believe that most independent schools (and non-maintained special schools) will wish to follow the line required of LEA maintained and grant-maintained schools' (DES, 1987, p.15). Why has this distinction been made? Why should pupils in independent schools not be required to follow the national curriculum and be tested at seven, eleven, fourteen and sixteen? After all, the consultation document asserts the Government's conviction that 'pupils should be entitled to the same opportunities wherever they go to school, and standards of attainment must be raised throughout England and Wales' (DES, 1987, p.3). What concept of a national curriculum and of a national education, indeed what concept of a nation underlies this document? Is it that teachers in independent schools can be trusted to provide a balanced curriculum and appropriate standards of education whilst teachers in state schools can not? Is it that pupils in independent schools can be trusted to make the right choice of subjects and to work hard, whilst those in state schools can not? Is this an attempt to hold down standards in independent schools? Is the purpose of this document and proposed legislation to promote a widening of those curricular and broader educational differences which have been such a recurring feature of education in this country since the nineteenth century? Are independent schools to be above the law? Apparently so, for it is reported from the DES that 'the Government believe it would not be right to impose the national curriculum on independent foundations' (*The Guardian,* 22 September 1987).

In the nineteenth century some Conservative politicians, including Disraeli, saw the division of British society into 'two nations' and recognized the need to close the gap. The leading exponent of Tory reform in education was Sir John Pakington, MP for Droitwich from 1837 to 1874, and subsequently raised to the peerage as Baron Hampton. Pakington's unsuccessful education bills of 1855 and 1857 both included provision for a broad curriculum in elementary schools, whilst in 1865 he gave evidence to the Taunton Commission both on the need for the modernization of grammar school curricula and for a mix of social classes in schools. In 1862 in a presidential address to the Birmingham and Midland Institute, Pakington contrasted the curriculum of the Institute favourably with that of the Public Schools.

When I see that, after your periodical examinations, certificates have been granted to very many candidates of chemical physics, elementary chemistry, analytical chemistry, English history and literature, the French and German languages, English grammar and composition, geometry, algebra and advanced arithmetic, I cannot refrain from comparing such a course of study with the teaching given in our great public schools to the sons of the highest and wealthiest citizens of the State (Aldrich, 1979, p.23).

Pakington's preference for a modern as opposed to a traditional curriculum was not shared by those who controlled nineteenth-century education, and was in advance of the thinking of those who framed the secondary school regulations of 1904. Morant's aim was to model the curriculum of the new secondary schools established under the 1902 Act not upon the scientific and technical work of the institutions and higher grade schools but upon the academic and literary approach of the Public Schools. Though the 1904 Regulations prescribed a much broader curriculum than that which had existed in the nineteenth-century Public Schools, as Eaglesham has rightly concluded, 'they certainly effectively checked any tendencies to technical or vocational bias in the secondary schools' (Eaglesham, 1967, p.59).

The choices made by such men as Morant and Headlam in the first decade of the twentieth century when the prime purpose of secondary education was to produce a ruling elite who could command authority both at home and in the world's largest empire were understandable. Morant, the permanent secretary of the Board of Education had been educated at Winchester and Oxford where he read Greats and theology. Headlam, an influential HMI who produced a highly critical report on the teaching of literary subjects in ex-higher grade secondary schools, was a product of Eton and Cambridge, where he studied Classics, and a former professor of Greek and Ancient History. They were thus products of the Clarendon Public Schools and of Oxbridge, as are Sir Keith Joseph and Kenneth Baker who both graduated from Magdalen College, Oxford, having been schooled at Harrow and St. Paul's respectively. Their experiences, values, priorities and judgements in respect of curriculum were seriously limited even in 1904. In 1988 the nation, national education and a national curriculum cannot be built upon so limited a foundation.

IV

The term 'curriculum' is not easily defined, but one of the most striking features of the consultation document is the fact that curriculum is prescribed in terms of subjects. True, some flexibility is to be allowed in organizing the school day and in teaching, and 10-20 per cent of the week or more may be used for other types of study, although once again these are defined for years 4 and 5 in secondary schools as 'additional subjects' (DES, 1987, p.6). Nevertheless, whether in primary or secondary schools, when it comes to the crunch 'The clear objectives for what pupils should be able to know, do and understand will be framed in subject terms' (DES, 1987, p.9). There is little place, if any, therefore, for the interpretation of the Hadow Report of 1931 which advised that 'the curriculum is to be thought of in terms of activity and experience rather than of knowledge to be acquired and facts to be stored' (Board of Education, 1931, p.93). Nor does any account seem to have been taken of Paul Hirst's 'forms of knowledge', of Denis Lawton's 'core areas of knowledge', nor even of Her Majesty's Inspectors' 'areas of experience', all of which have sought to redefine the school curriculum in other than subject terms.

Not only is no awareness shown of non-subject approaches, the very list of subjects virtually mirrors that of 1904. Have there been no additions to knowledge since that date? Are economics, business studies, commercial skills, social studies, health education, personal and social educational programmes, life skills programmes of the type developed by the Associated Examining Board, and a host of others, to be squeezed into a mere 10 per cent of time? Will children be required to continue to learn a foreign language, for example at the age of sixteen, at the expense of other studies in which they are both competent and interested, and which have immediate vocational relevance? Has any account been taken of the interests of parents and pupils in curriculum formulation? In 1968 the Schools Council *Enquiry 1* reported the considerable mismatch which existed between the purposes of secondary schools as seen by young school leavers and their parents on the one hand, and by head teachers and teachers in these schools on the other (Schools Council, 1968, pp.31-45). Will such difficulties be resolved by the imposition or re-imposition of an academic, subject-based curriculum?

V

Three points may be made in conclusion.

Central authority has a role to play in matters of curriculum, both as a partner in a shared process of curriculum construction and evaluation, and as an avenue of appeal against unreasonable action by local authorities and schools. On the other hand, central imposition of curriculum, particularly when subordinated to a crude policy of testing and resource limitation, has inflicted severe damage on the country's educational system in the past and has the potential to do so again. There are good grounds for arguing that the imposition itself and the specific curriculum proposed will hinder rather than advance individual and national development.

Similarly, central authority has a role to play in matters of standards and testing. For example, it is the duty of central government, as of other partners in the education service, to ensure that the consistent rise in levels of performance in external secondary school examinations over the last ten years is maintained. Such figures represent continuous improvement, and may be contrasted, for example, with those of industrial production or unemployment over the same period. There is some danger that a crude system of national testing imposed in defiance of professional advice may inhibit rather than secure further advance.

Finally, there are the warnings of Mr. Baker's predecessors. In 1870 W.E. Forster, Vice President of the Committee of Council for Education in Gladstone's first government rejected the idea of a centralized educational system on two grounds. In introducing his education bill he declared that the existing central educational authority did not have enough power to create and control such a system, and that to give it such power would be to call into being a potential tyranny.

Lord Eustace Percy, President of the Board of Education in Baldwin's Conservative government, 1924-9, resisted the arguments of critics within his own party who were calling for closer control of teachers and curriculum with the warning that nothing could be worse 'than to encourage a conception that teachers are servants of a Government in the same way as Civil Servants and therefore must teach in their schools precisely what any future Labour Government may tell them to teach . . .' (Lawn and Grace, 1987, p.206).

Let the final word rest with Sir Keith Joseph. On 10 February 1984 in a speech to the Historical Association in London he declared, 'It is no part of the responsibilities of the holder of my office to put forward a single model curriculum for all our schools' (*The Historian*, 1984, Vol.2, p.10).

References

Aldrich, R. (1979), *Sir John Pakington and National Education.* Leeds: University of Leeds.

Board of Education (1905, 1929, 1937), *Handbook of Suggestions for the Consideration of Teachers and others concerned with the Work of Public Elementary Schools.* London: HMSO.

——— (1931), *Report of the Consultative Committee on the Primary School.* London: HMSO.

Department of Education and Science (1985), *Better Schools,* Cmnd. 9469, London: HMSO.

——— (1987), *The National Curriculum 5-16, a consultation document,* London: DES.

Eaglesham, E. (1967), *The Foundations of Twentieth-Century Education in England.* London: Routledge and Kegan Paul.

Gordon, P. and Lawton, D. (1978), *Curriculum Change in the Nineteenth and Twentieth Centuries.* Sevenoaks: Hodder and Stoughton.

Lawn, M. and Grace, G. (eds.) (1987), *Teachers: the culture and politics of work.* Basingstoke: Falmer Press.

Schools Council (1968), *Enquiry 1.* London: HMSO.

Wiener, M. (1981), *English Culture and the Decline of the Industrial Spirit, 1850-1980.* Cambridge: Cambridge University Press.

Two Models of a National Curriculum: origins and interpretation

Clyde Chitty

Much of the problem of debating curriculum issues centres on the question of definitions. Over the past twenty years, there has been talk of an integrated curriculum (Lawton, 1969), a compulsory curriculum (White, 1973), a common culture individualized curriculum (Lawton, 1973), a common curriculum, a core curriculum, a common-core curriculum and now, finally, a national curriculum. The impression has often been created that these all amount to the same thing which is, in fact, very far from the truth.

In the context of this present publication, I have space to deal with only two of the models outlined above. I intend to examine the discernible origins of the professional common-curriculum model put forward by, among others, a group of Her Majesty's Inspectors and of the bureaucratic core-curriculum model advocated over the years by the civil servants of the Department of Education and Science. I shall tend to concentrate on the earlier manifestations of these models in the 1970s and early 1980s, leaving other contributors to focus on more recent developments. But it is important to be clear, at the outset, about the underlying assumptions of the two concepts.

As has been argued elsewhere (Lawton and Chitty, 1987), the professional common-curriculum approach, as exemplified in the three HMI Red Books published between 1977 and 1983 (DES, 1977b; 1981b; 1983), reflects a genuine concern with the quality of the teaching process and with the needs of individual children. It seeks to undermine traditional subject boundaries and uses subjects to achieve higher level aims. It requires teachers who are well-motivated, well-trained, and skilled in identifying any specific learning problems for individual pupils. It is wary of any system geared to writing off large sections of the school population as failures.

The bureaucratic core-curriculum approach, on the other hand, is concerned with the 'efficiency' of the whole system and with the need to obtain precise information to demonstrate that efficiency. It is concerned with controlling what is taught in schools and making teachers generally more accountable for their work in the classroom. Whereas the professional approach focuses on the quality of input and the skills, knowledge and awareness of the teacher, the bureaucratic approach concentrates on output and testing. Whereas the professional approach is based on individual differences and the learning process, the bureaucratic approach is associated with norms or bench-marks, norm-related criteria and judgements based on the expectations of how a statistically-normal child should perform. Whereas the professional curriculum is concerned with areas of learning and experience, the bureaucratic curriculum is preoccupied with traditional subject boundaries.

The HMI model

Much of the writing about the national curriculum debate appears to suggest that it all began with James Callaghan's Ruskin College Speech of October 1976 and the so-called 'Great Debate' which followed it in 1977. Yet it is important to establish that HMI interest in whole-school curriculum policies goes back further than 1976.

We learn from Red Book Three, *Curriculum 11-16: towards a statement of entitlement,* that it was in April 1975 that a group of HMI was concerned 'to develop ideas within the Inspectorate about the nature and purposes of the curriculum for pupils aged eleven to sixteen' (DES, 1983, p.1). In fact, HMI had taken on a planning role with regard to the secondary curriculum the year before, when Sheila Browne became Senior Chief Inspector. And we can go back even further than 1974.

Schools Council Working Paper 33, *Choosing a Curriculum for the Young School Leaver,* provides a revealing account of the Scarborough Conference of June 1969 where at least one of the discussion groups (which included an HMI representative) was beginning to question the Schools Council's piecemeal approach to curriculum planning.

[A] major problem to be faced was whether we were giving so much freedom to each individual school that continuity for our pupils in a mobile society was ignored. In fact, do we not have so many *general* curricular questions to answer that there ought to be a project on the curriculum *as a whole?* Are we right to be jiggling with the pieces in order to find new ways of putting them together? Is there a need to look at the whole conception for secondary education, and would this help heads to make their choices? . . . One group, in defining the curriculum, was moving towards considerations of this kind, while an HMI representative pointed out that there was a group in the Inspectorate already giving it serious thought. He defined the essentials of a good curriculum as giving importance to personal development, aesthetic experience, experience of the material world and of society, and 'transcendentalism' — ideals and inspiration (Schools Council, 1971, p.26).

The timing here is significant. The late 1960s marked the end of a period of ten or more years which has been described by Lawton and Gordon (1987, p.24) as 'probably . . . the lowest period of HMI influence and morale'. For one thing, there was the continuing problem of overlap between HMI and local authority inspectors; and HMI themselves felt that their professional expertise was not making itself felt. In an interview with Maurice Kogan published in 1971, Edward Boyle, who had served at the Ministry of Education in 1957-9 and 1962-4, conceded that the civil servants had not always made effective use of the professional knowledge of HMI:

> Looking back over the period we're thinking of, about fifteen years, the Inspectorate has played less of a part in policy making than I for one would have liked to see . . I don't think there was a sufficiently strong tradition that when you had a major discussion the Senior Chief Inspector should normally be invited in . . . I think there may have been personal reasons over the years why this tended not to happen. But, for whatever reason, he didn't play a big enough part in the Department, whoever he was (Boyle and Crosland, 1971, pp.130-1).

The findings of the 1967-8 Parliamentary Select Committee which scrutinized the work of HMI made it clear that there was a desperate need for HMI to find a new role and one, moreover, which did not duplicate the work of LEA advisory services. And the document *HMI Today and Tomorrow,* published in 1970, can perhaps be seen as an attempt by the Inspectorate to justify its very existence — an attempt, so to speak, at self-promotion. That justification was to be provided by the pursuit of a number of new strategies, foremost among them being the planning of a common culture curriculum. By the mid-1970s, this work was taking place alongside DES attempts to formulate a core curriculum of its own.

Within eighteen months, the group of HMI convened in April 1975 to develop ideas on the secondary curriculum (known as the Curriculum Publications Group) had produced a series of draft papers which were then offered as an HMI contribution to a DES conference on 'The secondary curriculum', held at the University of Oxford in September 1976. These papers were to form the nucleus of Red Book One, *Curriculum 11-16*, which, though dated December 1977, was not, in fact published until March 1978.

In one of his introductory papers for the Oxford Conference, R.A. Wake of the CPG conceded that there was still a basic need in England to arrive at some sort of agreement about the aims and objectives of the secondary curriculum:

> A major element in a 'national debate' on secondary education is that there is no easily discernible consensus within schools, let alone outside them, about the purposes of the curriculum. From this never-ending world of argument — much of it understandably low level — comes demands for 'a survival kit curriculum'. This infers that we should arrive at a national consensus about the essentials that should be in all secondary curricula: essential knowledge; essential skills.

Following on from this, it was emphasized that the CPG preferred a common 11-16 curriculum to be followed, for at least two-thirds of the time, by all pupils. Moreover, traditional subjects would be considered useful only to the extent that they contributed to the education of each individual pupil in the light of a checklist of areas of personal development or experience to be used as the basis of curriculum construction.

As a result of the Oxford Conference, a decision was taken to establish an exercise on curricular enquiry in which a small number of schools would join LEA advisers and HMI in reviewing their own curricula using the checklist drawn up by the CPG. Five local authorities, Cheshire, Hampshire, Lancashire, Nottinghamshire and Wigan, agreed to join HMI in this exercise, involving teachers from forty-one schools. Work began in 1977, with participants using the draft HMI papers, then unpublished, as an initial stimulus to their thinking and work (DES, 1983, p.1).

Red Book One, published in 1978, made the ideas of the CPG available to a wider audience. Yet by that time, the idea of a common or common-core curriculum had become associated with the suspicion that the Government was primarily concerned to bring about greater control of education. Accordingly, the authors of the Red Book felt it necessary to assert right at the outset that their ideas should be judged on their merits as *curriculum* proposals:

> These papers have been overtaken by events, and it is important that neither their content nor their purpose should be misunderstood . . . There is no intention anywhere in the papers which follow of advocating a centrally controlled or dictated curriculum . . The group of HM Inspectors who wrote these papers felt that the case for a common curriculum, as it is presented here, deserves careful attention and that such a curriculum, worked out in the ways suggested, would help to ameliorate the inconsistencies and irrationalities which at present exist, without entailing any kind of centralized control (DES, 1977b, p.1).

As foreshadowed in the draft papers for the Oxford Conference, the Red Book put forward a checklist of eight 'areas of experience', to be used as the basis of curriculum construction or of reshaping and redefining existing curricula:

- The aesthetic and creative
- The ethical
- The linguistic
- The mathematical

- The physical
- The scientific
- The social and political
- The spiritual (ibid., p.6).

This checklist could be translated into a timetable for the older pupils in a comprehensive school in the following way:

Subject	Periods	
English	5	
Mathematics	5	
A modern language	4	
A science	5	
Religious education and a social study	4	
Art/Craft/Music	4	
Careers education	2	
Physical activities	3	(ibid., p.7)

Based on a forty-period week, it would correspond to the HMI estimate that the common curriculum should occupy two-thirds or more of the total time available. The eight remaining periods could then be used for the provision of two further option blocks, allowing pupils to choose additional subjects (for example: a second foreign language or a classical study or another science) or to devote more time to subjects already being studied.

Yet the authors of the Red Book make it clear that, in its crude form, this model falls far short of what they would want to see in practice. Such curriculum construction in terms of subjects is acceptable when, but only when, everyone is clear what is to be achieved through them:

> It is . . . important to emphasize the fact that subject or 'course' labels often tell us surprisingly little about the objectives to be pursued or the activities to be introduced, still less about the likely or expected levels of achievement. An individual subject may make valid, although varied, contributions in different schools; or to different pupils in the same school; or to the same pupils at different ages or stages of individual development. Any framework to be constructed for the curriculum must be able to accommodate shifts of purpose, content and method in subjects, and of emphasis between subjects. In other words, it is not proposed that schools should plan and construct a common curriculum in terms of subject labels only: that would be to risk becoming trapped in discussions about the relative importance of this subject or that. Rather, it is necessary to look through the subject or discipline to the areas of exprience and knowledge to which it may provide access, and to the skills and attitudes which it may assist to develop (ibid., p.6).

By 1983 and the publication of Red Book Three, the final report of the enquiry which began in 1977, HMI were talking in terms of an 'entitlement curriculum' — a broad framework representing a synthesis of the vocational, the technical and the academic:

> It seemed essential that *all* pupils should be guaranteed a curriculum of a distinctive breadth and depth to which they should be *entitled,* irrespective of the type of school they attended or their level of ability or their social circumstances and that failure to provide such a curriculum is unacceptable . . . The conviction has grown that all pupils are entitled to a broad compulsory common curriculum to the age of sixteen which

introduces them to a range of experiences, makes them aware of the kinds of society in which they are going to live and gives them the skills necessary to live in it. Any curriculum which fails to provide this balance and is overweighted in any particular direction, whether vocational, technical or academic, is to be seriously questioned. Any measures which restrict the access of all pupils to a wide-ranging curriculum or which focus too narrowly on specific skills are in direct conflict with the entitlement curriculum envisaged here (DES, 1983, pp.25, 26).

The DES model

The DES concept of a core curriculum, which is the other main concern of this chapter, has always differed from the common curriculum model advocated by HMI in a number of significant ways: it still permits a fair amount of pupil choice, being little more in years four and five than a variation of the 'core-plus-options' syndrome; and it is conceived of primarily in terms of traditional subjects.

Of course, the idea of a core curriculum is not itself new. In the inter-war years, the curriculum in all secondary schools was tightly controlled, not only by the Secondary Regulations but also by the fact that most pupils were expected to take the School Certificate examination. The School Certificate was a group examination requiring at least five passes including English. In effect, all secondary schools worked with a core curriculum which, though established by the Regulations, was, in fact, implemented by the structure of a group examination. This ended only because the Secondary Regulations were made obsolete by the 1944 Education Act and the School Certificate was replaced, in 1951, by the new single-subject GCE Ordinary level examination. By the early 1950s, most grammar schools had abandoned any idea of a core or common-core curriculum.

Many of the secondary modern schools which grew up in the 1940s and 1950s experimented with basing their curriculum on social studies as the dominating core to which everything else then had to be subservient. As Cannon has shown, such schemes failed for a number of reasons, not least the need for schools to be seen to be achieving good examination results in a variety of subjects:

Most important probably were the social and economic pressures which led to an increasing concern for standards, and, in particular, to their expression in examination qualifications (Cannon, 1964, p.22).

The idea of some sort of core curriculum was revived by the civil servants of the DES in the confidential Yellow Book prepared within the Department in 1976. However, no attempt was made to define the term; and the paragraph in question is remarkable for its blandness and imprecision:

> . . . An analysis of the courses followed by individual pupils in school, particularly perhaps the most and least able, would reveal causes for dissatisfaction in terms of the general balance of their studies. The time has probably come to try to establish generally accepted principles for the composition of the secondary curriculum for all pupils, that is to say a 'core curriculum'. One advantage of the existence of such a curriculum would be its guarantee of relative continuity to children moving between schools in different parts of the country. The creation of a suitable core curriculum will not, however, be easy. Pupils in their later years of secondary schooling (up to and beyond the age of compulsory attendance) have a wide range of interests and expectations, and suitable provision will have to be made for vocational elements within school education for those who will benefit from this. Extensive consideration and consultation will be needed before a core curriculum could be introduced (DES, 1976, p.11).

The 'core curriculum' idea was taken up by Prime Minister James Callaghan in his Ruskin College Speech of October 1976 which, contrary to popular belief, was prepared not within the DES but by Bernard Donoughue and others of the Downing Street Policy Unit (Callaghan, 1987, p.410; Donoughue, 1987, p.111). It nevertheless covered many of the issues and shared many of the assumptions to be found in the DES Yellow Book. The curriculum was listed as one of the fields that 'need study because they cause concern':

> They are the methods and aims of informal instruction; the strong case for the so-called 'core curriculum' of basic knowledge; next, what is the proper way of monitoring the use of resources in order to maintain a proper national standard of performance; then there is the role of the inspectorate in relation to national standards, and there is the need to improve relations between industry and education (reprinted in *Education,* 22 October 1976, pp.332-3).

As promised in the Speech, a number of these issues were taken up by Secretary of State Shirley Williams and found their way into the Green Paper published in July 1977. Here it was argued that the curriculum had become overcrowded, with too much variation between schools:

. . . It is clear that the time has come to try to establish generally accepted principles for the composition of the secondary curriculum for all pupils. This does not presuppose uniform answers: schools, pupils and their teachers are different, and the curriculum should be flexible enough to reflect these differences. But there is a need to investigate the part which might be played by a 'protected' or 'core' element of the curriculum common to all schools. There are various ways this may be defined. Properly worked out, it can offer reassurances to employers, parents and the teachers themselves, as well as a very real equality of opportunity for pupils (DES, 1977a, p.11).

Clearly, little agreement had yet been reached on the actual composition of the core, though reference is made in the Green Paper to five subjects which would seem to have a right to be included:

English and religious education are in most schools a standard part of the curriculum for all pupils up to the age of sixteen, and it is not true that many pupils drop mathematics at an early stage . . . Few, inside or outside the schools, would contest that alongside English and mathematics, science should find a secure place for all pupils at least to the age of sixteen, and that a modern language should do so for as high a proportion as practicable (ibid., p.11).

The 'core curriculum' concept was developed further in two DES documents: *A Framework for the School Curriculum,* published in January 1980, and *The School Curriculum,* published in March 1981. The first of these documents went so far as to specify what proportion of time should be spent on some subjects, though this idea was repudiated in the following terms a year later:

English, mathematics, science and modern languages are generally treated as separate items in school timetables . . . The Secretaries of State do not suggest minimum times which should be devoted to these subjects. Any suggested minima might too easily become norms, or be interpreted too rigidly. It is for the local education authorities to consider, in consultation with the teachers in their areas, whether to suggest minimum time allocations in these subjects as broad guidance for schools (DES, 1981a, p.14).

These documents provoked lively controversy as to the merits and defects of a 'core curriculum' framework. Yet by the early 1980s, curriculum matters had become inextricably linked with the issues of central control of education and the vocationalization of the curriculum. As a result, it was often very difficult for both DES and HMI arguments to penetrate the resistance of a teaching profession anxious to guard its frail autonomy.[1]

The 1987 national curriculum

At first sight, the recently-published consultation document (DES, 1987) would appear to be in direct descent from the DES curriculum documents of the late 1970s and early 1980s. It certainly shows little sign of being influenced by the strongly liberal-humanist views of HMI, and has been severely criticized by teachers and educationists for its narrow, subject-based instrumental approach. As Lawton has pointed out (1987):

> There is nothing wrong with subjects provided they are treated as means and not as ends. Virtually all the enlightened views on curriculum planning are now agreed that subjects should be regarded as important only if they help to reach other objectives which, in turn, have to be justified
> . . . All this is ignored in the consultation document: no justification is put forward for the selection of the foundation subjects; no argument put forward to give priority to the core subjects; no attempt made to relate subjects to wider objectives.

Similarly, the notion of ten foundation subjects has been characterized as both 'vague and mechanistic' in a letter to *The Independent* from a group of academics at the University of Sussex (Abbs et al., 1987):

> The subjects listed seem to be no more than lumps extracted from the curriculum *status quo* which the Government happens to approve of. What we need . . . is some appreciation of the broad unifying categories (humanities, arts, sciences) which, when placed properly together, might come to represent some kind of balance.

Having emphasized the continuing subject-based approach, it is also important to see how the document of July 1987 represents a curious departure from earlier DES offerings. For one thing, the core is defined more rigidly than one might have thought possible ten years ago. (Even *A Framework for the School Curriculum,* with its recommended time

---

1. The (temporary) convergence of HMI and DES views on curriculum matters in 1985 is discussed in Janet Maw's chapter, pp.54-5.

allocations for some subjects, had a core consisting of only five subjects: English, mathematics, science, religious education and physical education — with modern languages also being recommended for most pupils.) At the same time, there are few references in the 1987 document to the need for the curriculum to be made more relevant to adult and working life, a key concept which has found its way into all DES statements published since 1976 culminating with the appearance of *Better Schools* in March 1985.

In this last respect, it is useful to examine the treatment of the Technical and Vocational Education Initiative (TVEI) as indicative of the change in emphasis. This initiative, the brainchild in 1982 of a triumvirate consisting of David (now Lord) Young, Sir Keith Joseph and Norman Tebbit, was awarded many column inches in the 1985 White Paper:

. . . The TVEI embodies the Government's policy that education should better equip young people for working life. The courses are designed to cater equally for boys and girls across the whole ability range and with tedchnical or vocational aspirations, and to offer in the compulsory years a broad general education with a strong technical element followed, post-sixteen, by increasing vocational specialization. The course content and teaching methods adopted are intended to develop personal qualities and positive attitudes towards work as well as a wide range of competence, and more generally to develop a practical approach throughout the curriculum. The projects are innovative and break new ground in many ways, being designed to explore curriculum organization and development, teaching approaches and learning styles, co-operation between the participating institutions, and enhanced careers guidance supported by work experience, in order to test the feasibility of sustaining a broad vocational commitment in full-time education for fourteen-to-eighteen year olds (DES, 1985, pp.16-17).

In the 1987 document, however, TVEI warrants only two brief mentions:

. . . The Government intends that legislation should leave full scope for professional judgement and for schools to organize how the curriculum is delivered in the way best suited to the ages, circumstances, needs and abilities of the children in each classroom. This will, for example, allow curriculum development programmes such as the Technical and Vocational Education Initiative (TVEI) to build on the framework offered by the national curriculum and to take forward its objectives (paragraph 27).

and:

> . . . For the final two years of compulsory schooling, the national extension of TVEI will also help LEAs in the development and establishment of the national curriculum, particularly in the areas of science and technology and in enhancing the curriculum's relevance to adult and working life (paragraph 85).

Nowhere in the document, as Low has pointed out (1987), is there any mention of the many new subjects, such as hotel and food services, robotics, microelectronics or manufacturing technology, which teachers have been able to introduce — for at least some of their pupils — as part of the TVEI scheme. As I have argued elsewhere (Chitty and Worgan, 1987, p.33):

> It could well be that so much energy is now being devoted to undermining comprehensive education by the dismantling of the state system that there is less need to concentrate on initiatives designed to promote differentiation *within* existing schools.

If we are right in assuming — and at the moment we have to rely on informed speculation — that over the past year or so the DES and the Secretary of State have succumbed to the influence of such extremist groupings as the Hillgate Group and the Institute of Economic Affairs, then it could be argued that the whole idea of a *national* curriculum is both illogical and irrelevant — that interest in it, on the part of the Government is, in fact, half-hearted. It could be said to act as a sort of 'fig-leaf' for the more divisive features of the educational policy of the New Right. As such, it is part of a debate that the Government is no longer really interested in. A perceptive editorial in *The Times Educational Supplement* prior to the last election (22 May 1987) argued that the Labour and Alliance manifestos appeared to be trapped in a time-warp while the Government had embarked on a truly radical course of its own:

> There is a lot in the opposition party policies which reads like an intelligent commentary on *Better Schools*. They have done Sir Keith Joseph the honour of taking him seriously, only to find the Tories have got bored with the nuts and bolts of *Better Schools* and gone for the ideology of vouchers in all but name.

According to this analysis, the national core curriculum can be understood only in relation to the whole package of reforms outlined in the 1987 Conservative Party manifesto and later enshrined in the 1987 Reform Bill. If such a curriculum has any validity for the New Right, it is as justification for a massive programme of national testing at seven, eleven, fourteen and sixteen which will, in turn, result in differentiation, selection and streaming at both the primary and secondary levels. Indeed, the whole process of curriculum standardization and testing would be ideologically consistent with the rest of the education 'package' if it could be seen as providing evidence to parents for the desirability or otherwise of individual schools.

Conclusion

One is left at the end of this analysis with a profound sense of depression and foreboding. While the manner of bringing forward the new curriculum proposals is disturbing, the motives underlying them cause severe misgivings. It would appear that for some of the bureaucrats of the DES, the *fact* of control is far more important than the *form* of control; for others, all that matters is the privatization of the system along lines laid down by the Prime Minister and her ideological allies. Either way, a great opportunity has been lost. In the words of Peter Cornall, Senior County Inspector for Cornwall, speaking at the School Curriculum Development Committee's National Conference in Leeds in September 1987:

> Many of us have no quarrel with a largely common curriculum: on the contrary we have been trying for years to convert others by example. What we could not have foreseen is the manner in which all this is happening, a manner so ill-matched to an issue of such fundamental national importance. Surely the foundations of no lasting monument are laid in obscurity, by artificers whose credentials cannot be scrutinized? A forum much nearer in character to a Royal Commission, consisting of known persons, presenting a Report beyond all suspicion of partisan influence or short-term considerations, could have commanded support and goodwill, far beyond what even the most thorough and competent of Civil Service papers can expect to do. Instead, we have the gravely-flawed product of amateurs, a hasty, shallow, simplistic sketch of a curriculum,

reductionist in one direction, marginalizing in another, paying only a dismissive lip-service to the professional enterprise and initiative on which all progress depends (O'Connor, 1987, p.34).

It is, then, both sad and ironic that, ten years after the 'Great Debate' of 1976/77, we should be presented with a national curriculum framework which has so little to commend it, that it brings into disrepute the very concept of a common curriculum for the nation's schools.

References

Abbs, P. et al. (1987), 'Criticisms of the proposed national curriculum', *The Independent,* 14 October.

Boyle, E. and Crosland, A. (1971), *The Politics of Education.* Harmondsworth: Penguin.

Callaghan, J. (1987), *Time and Chance.* London: Collins.

Cannon, C. (1964), 'Social studies in secondary schools', *Educational Review,* Vol.17, pp.18-30.

Chitty, C. and Worgan, J. (1987), 'TVEI: origins and transformation', in C. Chitty (ed.), *Aspects of Vocationalism,* Post-Sixteen Education Centre, Institute of Education University of London.

Department of Education and Science (DES) (1970), *HMI Today and Tomorrow.* London: DES.

—— (1976), *School Education in England: problems and initiatives,* July.

—— (1977a), *Education in Schools: a consultative document* (Green Paper). London: HMSO, Cmnd. 6869.

—— (1977b), *Curriculum 11-16 (HMI Red Book One).* London: HMSO.

—— (1980), *A Framework for the School Curriculum.* London: HMSO.

—— (1981a), *The School Curriculum.* London: HMSO.

Department of Education and Science (1981b), *Curriculum 11-16: a review of progress* (HMI Red Book Two). London: HMSO.

——— (1983), *Curriculum 11-16: towards a statement of entitlement: curricular reappraisal in action* (HMI Red Book Three). London: HMSO.

——— (1987), *The National Curriculum 5-16: a consultation document.* London: DES, July.

Donoughue, B. (1987), *Prime Minister: the conduct of policy under Harold Wilson and James Callaghan.* London: Jonathan Cape.

Lawton, D. (1969), 'The idea of an integrated curriculum', *University of London Institute of Education Bulletin,* New Series, No.19, Autumn Term, pp.5-12.

——— (1973), *Social Change, Educational Theory and Curriculum Planning.* Sevenoaks: Hodder and Stoughton.

——— (1987), 'Fundamentally flawed', *The Times Educational Supplement,* 18 September.

Lawton, D. and Chitty, C. (1987), 'Towards a national curriculum', *Forum,* Vol.30, No.1, Autumn, pp.4-6.

Lawton, D. and Gordon, P. (1987), *HMI.* London: Routledge and Kegan Paul.

Low, G. (1987), 'Fall of the high-fliers', *The Observer,* 1 November.

O'Connor, M. (1987), *Curriculum at the Crossroads:* an account of the SCDC national conference on Aspects of Curriculum Change, University of Leeds, September, 1987. London: School Curriculum Development Committee.

Schools Council (1971), *Choosing a Curriculum for the Young School Leaver* (Working Paper No.33). London: Evans/Methuen.

White, J. (1973), *Towards a Compulsory Curriculum.* London: Routledge and Kegan Paul.

National Curriculum Policy: coherence and progression?

Janet Maw

In his speech to the Society of Education Officers in January 1987, Kenneth Baker said:

> As you know, I believe that, at least as far as England is concerned, we should now move quickly to a national curriculum. By that I mean a school curriculum governed by national criteria which are promulgated by the Secretary of State but in consultation with all concerned — inside and outside the educationd service, and are sufficiently flexible to allow schools and teachers to use professional enterprise and judgement in applying them to individual pupils in their particular schools. I want to finish up with criteria which are broadly accepted by those who have to apply them because they have had a say in their determination (DES, 1987c).

In the weeks that followed, leading to the general election in June, the idea of a national curriculum was fairly rapidly formulated into a more precise proposal, but incorporated into a general education 'package' whose other components — open enrolment, grant-maintained schools and financial devolution — appeared to be moving in a quite opposite direction to the centralization proposed for the curriculum. This education package was included in the 1987 Conservative Party election manifesto as a central plank.

Interviewed shortly before the 1987 election, Mr. Baker denied that he had been stampeded by right-wing elements in his party and claimed:

> The national core curriculum — that was my idea. At the time it was seen as very heretical. But in just a few months, all the political parties have come round to accepting it (*The Times Educational Supplement,* 5 June 1987).

Yet in the same interview he clearly implied a continuity of the recognition of both the need for change and its required direction. Referring to James Callaghan's recently published memoirs (Callaghan, 1987), he asked his interviewer:

> Have you read the Callaghan book? He realized that changes had to be made and he tried to fight back, but they thwarted him (ibid.)

It is not clear here whether the 'they' referred to is the Department of Education and Science bureaucracy or the wider educational establishment. What is clear is that Mr. Baker was claiming a parentage for his proposed changes in the actions of the previous Labour Government. After the election he continued his theme. The national curriculum, he claimed, in September 1987:

> . . . is not a sudden change of direction, but the natural next stage in what has been a process of evolution (*The Times Educational Supplement,* 25 September 1987).

In the same month, Angela Rumbold, speaking to the School Curriculum Development Committee's national conference in Leeds, made exactly the same claim: that this 'natural' evolutionary process had been 'hammered out' over the last ten years in policy statements, HMI documents, etc.

*   *   *

The import of such statements is clear. They attempt to establish that what is currently proposed regarding the national curriculum is the rational outcome of events initiated over a decade previously, by a different administration; they imply a consensus which enables opponents of the proposals to be presented as self-serving and complacent. There is undoubtedly a *prima facie* credibility to such claims. Callaghan's speech at Ruskin College in 1976 did signal a redefinition of the purposes of the education system away from a focus on the individual and towards a focus on the needs of society, interpreted more narrowly as the needs of the economy. The officially sanctioned concept of a core curriculum has certainly been with us since 1976. For instance, the confidential memorandum to Callaghan from the DES prior to the Ruskin speech said:

> The time has probably come to try to establish generally accepted principles for the composition of the secondary curriculum for all pupils, that is to say, a 'core curriculum' (DES, 1976, p.11).

The impression of continuity is reinforced by the fact that the set of aims first stated (but not defended) in the 'leaked' DES memorandum of 1976, reappeared subsequently in modified forms in documents ranging from Shirley Williams' Green Paper *Education in Schools* (DES 1977a) to Sir Keith Joseph's policy statement *Better Schools* (DES 1985c) nearly a decade later. In 1985, Eric Bolton, Senior Chief HMI, spoke of the 'unstoppable momentum' towards a common core curriculum (*The Times Educational Supplement*, 8 March 1985). More recently, a MORI/TES poll, reported in the same week as the general election of 1987, claimed that 80 per cent of the sample interviewed wanted a common core curriculum from five to sixteen, a similar poll in 1979 having recorded a majority in favour (*The Times Educational Supplement*, 12 June 1987).

However, it is one thing to be able to discern a developing trend; it is quite another to claim that a particular outcome in terms of a national curriculum and a particular process for arriving at it are the natural and rational result foreshadowed by previous events. This chapter aims to demonstrate that, whilst since 1979 there has been a degree of inconsistency and arbitrariness in Conservative policy on or affecting the school curriculum, the new Education Reform Bill represents a severe rupture in policy on both content and control, confusing and demoralizing to what were previously considered as 'partners' in the education service. I shall not consider the Labour administration before 1979 in any detail because, whilst recognizing that there was no sharp break in that year, nevertheless, the Labour Government produced no policy statement to follow the Green Paper. From 1977 the local education authorities were preparing their replies to Circular 14/77 (DES, 1977b) which requested certain information about their curriculum policies. Although *Local Authority Arrangements for the School Curriculum* (DES, 1979) demonstrated that many of those replies were, as was remarked at the time, 'politely worded nil returns', the general election forestalled a response by the Labour Government by removing it from power.

* * *

The first Conservative policy document to appear after the election was *The School Curriculum* (DES, 1981a). For the purposes of this analysis it was important in two ways. First of all, it demonstrated that the ideological differences within the DES, revealed by earlier papers, had not been reconciled. In 1980 the DES consultation paper *A Framework for the School Curriculum* (DES, 1980s) showed an instrumental and managerialist approach to the school curriculum (it was the first paper to suggest specified amounts of time for certain subjects), and its focus was on certain core subjects rather than on a common curriculum. On the other hand, the HMI consultation paper of the same year, *A View of the Curriculum,* put forward a strongly liberal-humanist rationale for a common curriculum based upon the pupils' right of access, and argued against 'an excessively instrumental view of the compulsory period of education' (DES, 1980b, p.15). This approach has been developed by HMI in the series of 'Red Books' (DES, 1977c; DES, 1981b; DES, 1983a), and is encapsulated in the sub-title to the third: *Towards a Statement of Entitlement.* These differences in perspective meant that in terms of curriculum content, *The School Curriculum* was somewhat schizophrenic in its proposals. Nevertheless, whilst these ideological differences are important, it is also important to recognize the strong consensus between HMI and civil servants that an increase in central control was necessary; a basis for negotiation therefore existed.

The second salient feature of *The School Curriculum,* as central as its view of the curriculum, is its policy on curriculum control. Following the arguments that changes in technology and the economy require changes in the content, quality and orientation of schooling, the paper continues:

> This calls, not for a change in the statutory framework of the education service, but for a reappraisal of how each partner in the service should now discharge those responsibilities assigned to him by law. The Secretaries of State consider that curriculum policies should be developed and implemented *on the basis of existing statutory relationships* between the partners and that this process must be based upon a clear understanding of and pay proper regard to the responsibilities and interests of each partner and the contribution that each can make (DES, 1981a, p.2).

The responsibilities of the Secretary of State and the LEAs are then specified. This statement is important. Comments that followed *The School Curriculum* focused largely on the novelty (and undesirability) of government and LEA intervention in the curriculum. But, with hindsight, perhaps what was more important was the degree of continuity implied. The concept of *partnership* is embodied in the document, but now extended from provision and administration to curriculum matters. No one partner is to dominate:

> Neither the Government nor the local authorities should specify in detail what the schools should teach (DES, 1981a, p.3).

No serious challenge to the legal position put forward in *The School Curriculum* was made at the time. Criticism tended to concentrate on the curriculum proposals (for example, in White et al., 1981).

A reinforcement of this concept of continuing partnership was the issuing of Circular 6/81 (DES, 1981c) in October 1981, asking the local authorities to review and plan the development of their curriculum policies 'in the light of what is said in *The School Curriculum'*, and in consultation with the schools. In December 1983 this was followed by Circular 8/83 (DES, 1983b), giving a more detailed specification of the information requested, to be submitted by the end of April 1984. This circular indicated that, whilst it was expected that LEAs would develop their plans *within* the national policy, at the same time the Secretary of State was to an extent dependent on them in carrying out his responsibilities, particularly in relation to school organization and the training of teachers. The circular concluded by indicating an ongoing process of consultation, publication and development of curriculum policies within the structure already defined.

During the period when the local authorities were being asked to develop and submit their policies, no further DES documents on the structure of the whole curriculum were published. But whilst it would be tempting to interpret this as illustrating the reality of consultation and partnership, it is notable that in these years the DES was in fact developing a whole series of powerful forms of *indirect* curriculum control. Taken together, increased resource control, control of teacher education (through the Council for the Accreditation of Teacher Education and grant-related in-service training), direct curriculum sponsorship (for example, Lower Attaining Pupils Programme), examination reform (CPVE, national criteria for the GCSE), policy-directed research funding, the abolition of the Schools Council and its replacement by two DES nominated bodies (the School Examinations Council and the School Curriculum Development Committee), and the TVEI, sponsored by the Manpower Services Commission, form, as I have previously suggested (Maw, 1985), a set of powerful constraints on the curriculum without forming a coherent framework for it. Indeed, some of these developments lead away from a common curriculum into differentiation and forms of selection via tracking, or different examinations. Arguments for inconsistency and arbitrariness in curriculum policy derive not only from an analysis of direct curriculum policy statements, but from seeing their relationship to other educational policies.

Another development during this period, with consequences for the future, was that HMI were continuing their collaborative exercise with five LEAs to develop a curriculum based on the ideas first presented in *Curriculum 11-16* (1977c) and further elaborated in the 'Red Books' of 1981 and 1983. This experience seems to have enabled HMI to sharpen and consolidate their thinking in the two areas of curriculum and control. We can trace through the 'Red Books' the development of a matrix view of the curriculum whereby content (classified as areas of experience) is set against the elements of learning (classified as knowledge, concepts, skills and attitudes), the whole organized by the principles of breadth, balance, relevance, coherence, progression and differentiation. The full statement of this framework eventually appeared in *Curriculum Matters 2, The Curriculum from 5 to 16* (DES, 1985a). On control, HMI conceptions of 'entitlement' had led them by 1983 to argue for a much more explicit, extensive and far-reaching specification of the entitlement curriculum than had previously been envisaged (DES, 1983a, pp.26-27). HMI do not state where and by whom this specification should be elaborated. However, it is quite logical to argue that if the entitlement is to be for all, then the specification should be made centrally. Some of the work of HMI, it can be argued, has provided ammunition for those wishing to follow its control implications whilst ignoring its curriculum structure and rationale.[1]

* * *

The local authorities replied to Circular 8/33 by the end of April 1984. A year later the most crucial recent policy statement on curriculum issues was published, *Better Schools* (DES, 1985c). This was an important document, not only for what was said, but also for what was implied. In particular, it indicated a greater convergence, or at least a willingness

---

1. The origins of HMI curriculum policy are traced in Clyde Chitty's paper.

to negotiate between HMI and DES officials. *Better Schools* gives HMI a strong role in the legitimation of its claims; there are four pages devoted to 'A professional judgement', which are entirely based on HMI evidence, particularly on evidence of weaknesses in the system (DES, 1985c, pp.4-8). There is a convergence of the language used. In addition, HMI are to have a strong role in curriculum development. Indeed, it is a confirmation of Salter and Tapper's thesis (Salter and Tapper, 1981) that in the drive towards centralization, a reorganized and more pliable HMI are to act as the 'organic intellectuals' of the DES, legitimating central intervention by providing justificatory information and by promulgating the correct curriculum message through their impeccably professional voice.

More explicitly, there is in *Better Schools* no mention at all of a national curriculum. Instead, we have the statement:

> Consultation with the Government's partners in the education service and with other interests have shown that there is widespread acceptance of the need to improve the standards achieved by pupils, and of the proposition that *broad agreement about the objectives and content of the school curriculum* is a necessary step towards that improvement (DES, 1985c, p.9) (my italic).

But the achievement of this 'broad agreement' through central compulsion is denied:

> . . . it would not, in the view of the Government be right for the Secretaries of State's policy for the range and pattern of the five-sixteen curriculum to amount to the determination of national syllabuses for that period (ibid, p.11).

The interrelationship of Government, LEAs and schools in the formulation of curriculum is reiterated:

> . . . the policies adopted at each level influence, and are influenced by, those adopted at others (ibid, p.10).

Within this framework, the Government's role in reaching this 'broad agreement' about the objectives and content of schooling (which it is acknowledged will take 'several years to accomplish') will be carried out through policy statements, such as *Science 5-16: a statement of policy* (DES 1985b), and through HMI publications:

. . . In particular publications in the recently inaugurated Curriculum Matters Series will build up a general description of the objectives of the curriculum as a whole for all children of compulsory school age (DES, 1985c, p.10).

This role for HMI in the progressive refinement and clarification of the curriculum is repeated in a section examining the contribution of subjects to the curriculum (ibid. p.18).

Finally, in relation to *Better Schools,* there is a strong reiteration of the statutory position regarding control of the curriculum that was first set out in *The School Curriculum* (DES, 1981a):

> The Government does not propose to introduce legislation affecting the powers of the Secretaries of State in relation to the curriculum (DES, 1985c, p.12).

and:

> The Government believes that the action now necessary to raise standards in school education can in the main be taken *within the existing legal framework,* which gives freedom to each LEA to maintain its existing pattern of school organization and, if it wishes, to propose changes in that pattern (ibid. p.63) (my italic).

The exception to this was seen to be the need to reform school governing bodies and clarify their functions. This was achieved through the Education Act 1986. As late as November 1985 the DES held a conference on evaluation and appraisal, as a follow-up to *Better Schools,* in which Sir Keith Joseph repeated the commitment to partnership, and the need to reach agreement over time (DES, 1986a, p.182).

*   *   *

The present far-reaching Education Reform Bill, presented to Parliament only ten months after a statutory national curriculum was announced as policy, represents, therefore, a most profound rupture with very recent policy statements from the present Government on both the content and control of the school curriculum. It is not a continuation; but the nature of the break is different. In curriculum we have a break with recent developments; in control, a break with a concept of shared, limited and balanced powers that has developed since the establishment of local education authorities in 1902.

In terms of curriculum content, the proposed national curriculum appears to run counter to both the differentiating tendencies of recent examination reform (indeed the consultation document *The National Curriculum 5-16* (DES, 1987a, p.10) specifically states that some GCSE criteria and syllabuses will need revising to bring them into line with the national curriculum) and the vocational thrust of such developments as the TVEI (mentioned only twice in the 1987 document). Reports of the threat to specific courses developed in response to vocational initiatives are already beginning to appear in the press (for example, in *The Times Educational Supplement,* 11 December 1987). However, the most notable omission in the consultation document is any reference to the curricular thinking of HMI. Their work since 1977 in the development of a curriculum framework is completely ignored, and instead of 'areas of experience' we have a list of subjects. To an extent, HMI can be blamed for this. They have never provided any philosophical ratinale for their 'areas of experience', and have altered and added to them over time without explanation. At the same time, the subject-specific 'Curriculum Matters' bulletins largely ignore the areas of experience. They are mentioned briefly only in those on Geography (DES, 1986b, pp.2-3) and Modern Languages (DES, 1987b, pp.2-3), and in neither case is there any attempt to explicate precisely how the subject contributes to the areas of experience. They can, therefore, be attacked as both theoretically suspect and practically irrelevant, and thus dismissed by the Secretary of State as 'education speak' (DES, 1987c, paragraph 11). Nevertheless, the complete eclipse of HMI in recent curriculum policy development appears to contradict Salter and Tapper's claim that:

> Any move by the DES to systematize further the process of policy construction is therefore dependent on HMI to acquire and disseminate the right information at the right time. This would imply that from the Department's point of view the closer the ties between itself and the HMI the better (Salter and Tapper, 1981, p.110).

Their strong role in ideological legitimation, so recently confirmed in *Better Schools,* has been negated. However, Salter and Tapper go on to say:

> Should the distinction between the Inspectorate and the DES become
> blurred in the eyes of the public, the role of HMI as the organic intellec-
> tuals wearing the appropriate ideological blanket to legitimate future
> policy will be seriously endangered (ibid, p.234).

One could argue, therefore, that current events imply as much an eclipse
of DES civil servants as of HMI, and we are witnessing the domina-
tion of the politicians. Mrs Thatcher's deep suspicion of DES officials
has been reported on a number of occasions, as has her determination
to oversee the passage of the Education Reform Bill (see, for example,
The Observer, 20 September 1987 and *The Times,* 15 October 1987);
and it is difficult to view its inconsistencies as the outcome of developed
policy advice from within the DES.

In terms of curriculum control a break with recent policy is also
apparent. Indeed the present Bill renders a considerable part of the *1986
Education Act* redundant. However, the real rupture in curriculum control is the break with the long tradition of partnership, and the clear
intention to reduce the role of local authorities to little more than that
of administering centrally-devised policies. The acquisition and centralization of control in the person of the Secretary of State is an
extraordinary development, given our history of suspicion of state
power in education. It has been argued that there is a tension in the
Bill between the centralized curriculum control proposed and the devolution of powers to schools, governors and parents. The tension is certainly there, but what is not so easily recognized is that the devolution
of powers, in itself, increases the powers of the Secretary of State,
because city technology colleges and grant-maintained schools will have
to deal directly with him. LEAs may wither away, but the DES bureaur-
carcy will certainly increase. During the Bill's second reading, Opposition education spokesperson Jack Straw pointed out that it gave the
Secretary of State 175 new powers (reported in *The Times Educational
Supplement,* 4 December 1987). The real danger that arises from this
is not totalitarianism, but politicization of the school curriculum. This
was pointed out in *The Times Educational Supplement* early in 1987.

> . . . nobody should be under any illusion that Labour would be anything
> but delighted if the Conservatives pave the way for a Government of
> the Left to reshape the school curriculum along lines acceptable to it (*The
> Times Educational Supplement,* 16 January 1987).

Be that as it may, there are certainly no adequate safeguards or constraints on such politicization if the Secretary of State has only to 'take note' of the advice of the National Curriculum Council, a body which he has nominated in the first place (*The Times Educational Supplement,* 27 November 1987).

* * *

How are we to understand this rupture, this volte face? Clearly one must be cautious in interpreting events which are both very recent, and about which the evidence available is still highly selective. Nevertheless, one can reject the explanation given or implied by Mr. Baker and his ministerial colleagues (for example, in Angela Rumbold's speech to the School Curriculum Development Committee's National Conference in September 1987) that consultation, clarification, persuasion and partnership have not worked, that little change has been effected. In the first place, the evidence prior to 1985 on which the claim might be made has not been published. We have no idea of the extent to which, for instance, the LEA responses to Circular 8/83 provided evidence of their developing policies in line with *The School Curriculum* or not. *Better Schools* tells us little on this issue. Whilst claiming that in secondary schools:

. . . there is little evidence of agreed curriculum policies directly influencing the school as a whole, in particular on such pervasive matters as the promotion of language development and careers education (DES, 1985c, p.7),

it also pays tribute to the local authorities:

. . . for the priority they have given to the formulation of curriculum policies over the past three years and more (ibid, p.12).

After listing the achievements, and the areas needing more attention, the document continues:

The responses show that an explicit curricular policy will shortly inform the work of nearly every LEA, but that many authorities' policies do not yet extend to all the matters for which local policies are needed (ibid, p.13).

This hardly indicates a failure to respond. Unfortunately, whilst *Better Schools* listed the publication of an account of LEA responses to circular 8/83 as one of the 'immediate tasks' for the Government, nearly three years later this publication has not appeared. However, it is too early to judge LEAs responses to *Better Schools* itself. Recently, HMI, in their review of provision for 1986 said:

> As in 1985, about a third of all authorities stated that they had an agreed curriculum for their school (HMI, 1987, p.28).

This does not accord with what was stated two years earlier in *Better Schools*. On the other hand, we should note that when the evidence for the HMI paper was being gathered, the 1986 Education Act had not yet come into force, only five of the HMI *Curriculum Matters* series had been published (one of which had to be revised due to extensive criticism from English teachers), and no further subject policy statements had appeared from the DES. It is not clear, therefore, precisely what LEAs and schools were supposed to be responding to after 1985.

At this point in time, two factors appear salient in evaluating curriculum policy changes. The first is simply political expediency, the need for an 'issue' around which to rally support during the election campaign. In the 1987 election, with no 'Falklands factor' to hand, education was tailor-made as an issue because the teachers' action and the activities of a small number of Labour LEAs allowed the Conservatives to launch a populist appeal on the slogans of 'standards' and 'choice'. In relation to the education package as a whole — opting out, budget devolution, and open enrolment — the national curriculum was central in enabling the Conservatives to claim a genuine concern for education, to deny that they were neglecting the many in favour of the few. This can be seen as a main reason for *having* a national curriculum, in opposition to the privatizing, differentiating tendencies of the rest of the package. Whilst not logically consistent, the national curriculum can be seen to have been politically necessary for the election campaign. Political expediency relevant to the exigencies of the election explains the speed of events, the lack of consultation, the frightening ignorance of Ministers of the implications of the policies they have set in motion (for instance in regard to the racial segregation of school), and their disagreements when such implications are pointed out (as reported, for example, in *The Times,* 14 November 1987 and *The Times Educational Supplement,* 20 November 1987). It also explains why, as late as December 1987, correspondents to the press were arguing that the complexities and contradictions of the Bill had not been thought through, least of all by those responsible for it (*The Times Educational Supplement,* 11 December 1987).

The second factor that appears to be important is that the Education Reform Bill, in its present form, is the outcome of ideological conflict, not *between* politicians, HMI and DES bureaucrats, but ideological conflict *within* the political Right in general, and the Conservative Party in particular. Here we must view the national curriculum proposals in relation to the whole Education Reform Bill, and the Bill in relation to such general Conservative policies as privatization. The internal evidence of the Bill itself demonstrates such conflict. The tensions between control and devolution, nationalization and privatization, uniformity and differentiation are inexplicable without such a concept. In addition there is plenty of external evidence. It is clear, for instance, that from the beginning of 1987 organizations of the Far Right, such as the Institute of Economic Affairs, the Centre for Policy Studies and the Hillgate Group were making strong efforts to influence Conservative education policy. In so far as their beliefs are in efficiency through competition (the operation of the 'market'), privatization, differentiation and ultimately selection, certain sections of the Bill, especially those relating to grant-maintained schools, represent success. However, within this scenario, to some of them the national curriculum is clearly an anomaly, a logical inconsistency. Thus Stuart Sexton a former adviser to Sir Keith Joseph, has recently argued:

> One of the Government's mistakes is over the national curriculum which is not a natural development from earlier Conservative policies and enactments . . . The nearest we need to a national curriculum is the reassertion of the three Rs on behalf of parents which was inherent in Sir Keith Joseph's paper *Better Schools* (Letter to *The Independent,* 19 November 1987).

In similar vein Dennis O'Keefe wrote earlier in the year;

> All the economic successes since 1979 have come from shifting power to the consumer and trusting markets to do the rest . . . The Government should have considered financial changes, such as tax relief which

would allow more parents effective rights of exit from the system: this would create competition and generate efficiency. The Government believes in capitalism. Why then does it favour coercive education? The surest advantage of markets is that they cannot be controlled politically (*The Times Educational Supplement,* 18 September 1987).

Mrs. Thatcher has been reported as being in sympathy with such views and as clashing with the Secretary of State on a number of matters, including the extent of the national curriculum, the extent of opting out to be considered desirable, the nature of testing, the reintroduction of selection, and responsibility for monitoring the system (as reported in *The Independent,* 21 September 1987; *The Observer,* 20 September 1987; and *The Times,* 18 October 1987). On all these matters she is further to the Right than Mr. Baker, who has been described as 'a liberal humanist fond of reading novels and reciting poetry' (*The Times Educational Supplement,* 9 October 1987). Certainly the proposed national curriculum is closer to the grammer school curriculum of 1904 than to any recent developments. Mr. Baker, then, can be seen as an inheritor of Raymond Williams' 'old humanists' (Williams, 1961, pp.161-165) who have always been strong in Conservative educational thinking, and for whom the prime functions of education are to civilize and moralize the young rather than to prepare them for future economic roles. Yet another Conservative perspective was represented recently by Edward Heath. Claiming Disraeli's 'one nation' view of the Conservative Party as his inspiration he attacked the social divisiveness inherent in the Bill (reported in *The Times,* 2 December 1987). Whilst no Conservative MP followed Heath in abstaining on voting at the second reading, others have been reported as concerned at the potential social backlash of this increasing divisiveness (*The Observer,* 22 November 1987). In addition, Heath's attack on the accrual of power to the Secretary of State makes common cause with the anti-state tradition of Conservative thinking which sees local control rather than market forces as the antidote to state power, and traces its ancestry at least as far back as the 'country party' of late seventeenth and early eighteenth-century politics. Currently of course, this tradition is powerful in Conservative local government, and it is clear that the present administration, heading a party that has always claimed to be the party of local government, is facing strong opposition not only from LEA administrators, but from Conservative local politicians whose perception is of a proud tradition threatened because of the antics of a minority on the Left. With so many cross-currents and conflicts within the Conservative Right, it is not possible at this stage to predict with confidence any precise outcome. However, those who have concentrated their attention on the curriculum proposals of the Bill might reflect that, if their concern is with the maintenance and development of an equitable, properly funded system of comprehensive schooling from five to sixteen, the worst possible outcome could be the total defeat of the national curriculum, whilst leaving the other proposals untouched. This would open the door to unfettered privatization, differentiation and selection.

References

Callaghan, J. (1987), *Time and Chance*. London: Collins.

Department of Education and Science (1976), *School Education in England: problems and initiatives*, July.

—— (1977a), *Education in Schools: a consultative document*. London: HMSO.

—— (1977b), Circular 14/77.

—— (1977c), *The Curriculum 11-16*. London: HMSO.

—— (1979), *Local Authority Arrangements for the School Curriculum: report of the 14/77 review*. London: HMSO.

—— (1980a), *A Framework for the School Curriculum*. London: HMSO.

—— (1980b), *A View of the Curriculum*. London: HMSO.

—— (1981a), *The School Curriculum*. London: HMSO.

—— (1981b), *Curriculum 11-16: a review of progress*. London: HMSO.

—— (1981c), Circular 6/81.

—— (1983a), *Curriculum 11-16: towards a statement of entitlement*. London: HMSO.

Department of Education and Science (1983b), Circular 8/83.

—— (1985a), *The Curriculum from 5 to 16* (Curriculum Matters 2.). London: HMSO.

—— (1985b), *Science 5-16: a statement of policy*. London: HMSO.

—— (1985c), *Better Schools*. London: HMSO.

—— (1986a), *Better Schools: evaluation and appraisal conference*. London: HMSO.

—— (1986b), *Geography from 5-16* (Curriculum Matters). London: HMSO.

—— (1987a), *The National Curriculum 5-16: a consultation document*. London: DES, July.

—— (1987b), *Modern Foreign Languages to 16* (Curriculum Matters 8.). London: HMSO.

—— (1987c), DES 22/87. 'Kenneth Baker calls for curriculum for pupils of all abilities.' Press Release.

Her Majesty's Inspectorate (1987), *Report by Her Majesty's Inspectors on LEA Provision for Education and the Quality of Response in Schools and Colleges in England, 1986*. London: DES.

Maw, J. (1985), 'Curriculum control and cultural norms: change and conflict in a British context', *New Era*, Vol.66, No.4.

Salter, B. and Tapper, T. (1981), *Education, Politics and the State*. London: Grant McIntyre.

White, J. et al. (1981), *No Minister: a critique of the DES paper 'The school curriculum'*. London: Institute of Education, University of London, Bedford Way Papers 4.

Williams, R. (1961), *The Long Revolution*. Harmondsworth: Penguin Books.

What Exams would mean for Primary Education

Caroline Gipps

The consultation document *The National Curriculum 5-16* (DES, 1987) makes it clear that the national curriculum is to be accompanied by examinations for primary school children at seven (or thereabouts) and eleven in the core subjects. The purpose of these is to assess the extent to which children have reached the benchmarks, or attainment targets, in the key subjects of English, maths and science. Attainment targets in other foundation subjects — history, geography and technology — may follow.

Much of the assessment at ages seven, eleven and fourteen (and at sixteen for non-examined subjects) will be done by teachers as part of normal classroom work.

> But at the heart of the assessment process there will be nationally pre-scribed tests done by all pupils to supplement the individual teachers' assessment. Teachers will administer and mark these, but their marking — and their assessments overall — will be externally moderated (DES, 1987, paragraph 29).

The tests will be developed by various organizations (presumably including the NFER and King's College London where Margaret Brown is already working on a feasibility study of differentiated attainment targets and tests in maths for the primary age) but administered and moderated by the five GCSE examining boards. Since these nationally prescribed tests are going to be under the aegis of the exam boards, and since they are going to assess performance in relation to a prescribed programme of work, in the way that public exams relate to a syllabus, I shall refer to them as exams. We might as well call a spade a spade, and this will help us to make clear what we mean and distinguish them from the tests which can be of teachers' own devising or the purchased tests which are commonly used to assess reading.

The aim of this chapter is to look at what the impact of these exams (and of the curriculum) is likely to be on primary education. Clearly the impact is a long way off, for the exams are unlikely to be in operation before 1991 and there is a major job to be done in developing them. Much of what I say will therefore be tentative, indeed speculative, and I make that clear at the start. However, it is not as speculative as all that, for we know what such a centralized examining system and curriculum mean for French and German primary schools, and we know what happens in this country and in the USA when testing is introduced. We also know what happened to primary education in this country when the eleven-plus examining system was curtailed and much of my analysis will draw on a comparison of primary education pre-and post-eleven-plus.

I think it is important to make this analysis now so that we can see more clearly where we are going. It may even be possible to have some small impact on the way the assessment system develops.

Background

Although the idea of examining in the primary school has come as something of a shock to those involved in primary education, we can in fact identify a history to the proposals. In October 1986, Kenneth Baker, Secretary of State for Education, said that he wished to see attainment targets for children of different ages developed on the grounds that they would help pupils to achieve the best performances they were capable of (reported in *The Times Educational Supplement,* 3 October 1986).

Mr Baker's view was foreshadowed by some comments of Eric Bolton (Senior Chief HMI) in November 1985:

> Much of the work on assessment and evaluation to date is biased towards the secondary phase. We lack broad agreement about how to describe and scrutinize the primary curriculum. The absence of clarity and agreement about what children should be capable of at various stages of their primary education leads to a distinct lack of information about standards

of pupil achievement in individual primary schools and a consequent difficulty of establishing any standards of achievement as a basis for an assessment of performance (reported in *The Times Educational Supplement,* 22 November 1985).

More recently, however, HMI have seemed a little ambivalent; some seem concerned about whether benchmarks would be helpful (see 'Benchmarks for reading "not helpful" says HMI', in *The Times Educational Supplement,* 20 February 1987), and about the dangers of introducing a national testing programme (see 'Chief HMI voices fears on national tests', in *The Times Educational Supplement,* 8 May 1987). To add to the confusion, the former Chief HMI for Primary Education, who thinks that widely accepted benchmarks would be helpful, has said that they do not need to be followed by mechanical testing (*The Times Educational Supplement,* 21 April 1987). Since he is a member of the Task Group on Assessment, it will be interesting to see how much influence he has on the shape of the final assessments.

The idea of attainment targets has, as Lawton points out,

all sorts of bureaucratic advantages in terms of presentation of statistics and making comparisons between teachers and schools. But age-related testing makes it very difficult to avoid normative procedures, norm-related criteria, and judgements based on the expectations of how a statistically-normal child should perform (Lawton, 1987).

Not only that, but attainment targets 'should cater for the full ability range' (DES, 1987, paragraph 23) and assess 'the knowledge, skills, understanding and aptitudes which pupils of different abilities and maturity should be expected to have acquired at or near certain ages' (ibid., Annex A). In other words they should be differentiated, just like the GCSE.

Understandably, there has been a considerable amount of concern voiced over the effect of testing younger children. But the current talk about benchmarks and national testing programmes makes it sound as though there is little testing within the primary range and that testing children at seven and eleven would be a new development. We have, however, evidence to show that this is simply not true: there is a considerable amount of testing going on in schools already at seven, eight *and* eleven.

The current state of testing in primary schools

In 1981 we carried out a survey of all LEAs asking about any testing
programmes they had, that is standardized tests of reading, maths, etc.
given routinely to all or part of an age group (Gipps et al., 1983). We
discovered that testing was widespread, with at least 79 per cent of LEAs
doing some kind of testing.

Testing at ages seven and eight was fairly common with 30 and 41
LEAs, respectively, giving reading tests at those ages. In addition, 14
LEAs gave maths tests and 12 gave reasoning tests [1] at eight; only 3
LEAs gave these latter two tests to seven year olds. There was some
testing at nine and ten, but the most common age for testing was eleven,
with 36 LEAs testing reading, 21 maths and 43 reasoning. In addition
86 per cent of schools in our survey used tests with whole age groups
on top of those required by the LEA. A further 7 per cent did not test
whole age groups but used tests with individual children. Only 7 per
cent of the schools (80 in all, chosen randomly from a stratified sample
of 20 LEAs) did not use standardized tests at all.

Towards the end of 1983, we sent another questionnaire to all LEAs,
this time asking specifically about screening programmes, that is tests
or checklists given routinely to all or part of an age group with the purpose of identifying children with special educational needs (Gipps et al.,
1987). Again, testing was widespread with 71 per cent of all LEAs having
at least one such programme.

Although this might look like a relative decline in the level of testing
since 1981, we cannot make this assumption, since in the two surveys
we were asking for different things: in the second survey we were asking specifically about screening programmes. These tend to be used at
younger ages and to involve reading tests more exclusively. We found
that 37 LEAs used tests or checklists at age seven, 36 at age eight, and
28 at age eleven. In addition, 18 LEAs screened at age five and 22 at
age six. So, yet again, the evidence showed that there was a great deal
of testing particularly in the seven and eight year groups.

We found very little evidence in the early 1980s that testing programmes, once instituted, were dropped. Once established they might
change, for example in age group covered or test used, but they were

---

1. Group tests of ability as used in the eleven-plus.

rarely abandoned. It is likely, therefore, that the amount of testing is little different now from that observed in 1981 and 1983. So we can see that testing is not unusual in primary schools. If, then, there is a good deal of testing going on in primary schools, what is it about the new proposals that is causing concern?

The proposals

There are three ways in which the new proposals are crucially different from current testing practices; the close links between the exams and the curriculum; the significance of the assessments; and their likely differentiated nature. These three points are, of course, common to formal public exams at secondary level.

The tests currently used most widely — that is, the standardized group reading and reasoning tests — are not related to the curriculum in primary schools; they float free of the curriculum rather than reflect it or control it. Maths tests used are either bought 'off-the-peg' from test publishers in which case they will reflect the curriculum only in a general way, or they are designed to go with LEA maths guidelines in which they will reflect the curriculum more specifically; the latter case, however, is less common. In the new proposals, on the other hand, exams are an essential part of the national curriculum; they are there to see that the curriculum is taught. With the old reading and reasoning tests it was not possible to teach to the test, by and large, nor was it necessary; with the new exams teachers will certainly, if not teach to the test, teach the given curriculum.

The significance of the new exams is likely to be different from that of the old LEA testing programmes. Results from the latter may have been used as part of the process to identify children with special needs, and in some, LEA advisory visits to offer professional support would follow poor results in a school. Apart from this, the major use of results was to be put in the record books to be passed on to the next teacher or school, or so that the LEA could say that it was doing something to 'monitor standards'. Their significance was strictly limited. Under the new proposals it is likely that the exams will be every bit as significant as those at sixteen-plus are now. Children will be classified much more formally on the basis of how they score on the exams and this will take place from the very beginning of the junior school. Since the results have to be made public, teachers will be under pressure to get good results not only for the children's benefit but for the school's (and of course their own). The London Borough of Croydon is currently unusual in making named school results available.

The new exams are not to be minimum competency tests on the popular American model, but differentiated, presumably along GCSE lines. This means that, either more able children will take harder papers than will the less able, or that all will take the same papers but differentiate themselves by their response. Either way, they are clearly not to be exams which everyone can pass equally well. Thus children will be classified according to how they performed on the papers. This classification may be only informal, in the teacher's head or record book, but Rosenthal and Jacobson's study showed us twenty years ago (Rosenthal and Jacobson, 1968) the impact that classification can have on children's future progress.

The classification will then be carried out again (and most probably confirmed) at eleven and this time, given the current plans for secondary education, the results are likely to be crucial in allocating children to, or allowing them to be selected for, different secondary schools: city technology colleges, comprehensives or grant-maintained schools.

The impact of exams on primary schools

We need first to consider what are the main features of primary education before we can begin to anticipate what impact exams and an assessment-led curriculum will have on primary education.

Armstrong has already said (Armstrong, 1987) that the effect 'will be to stifle innovation, to inhibit the free play of ideas and to extinguish any lingering sense of excitement, originality and adventure about the business of teaching and learning'. Broadfoot and Osborn who have made a comparative study of French and English school systems, found in French primary schools 'a dull, repetitive and harsh pedagogy' and suggest that teaching to the test will result in 'the sacrifice . . . of that warm and creative learning environment that has made English primary schooling the envy of many parts of the world' (Broadfoot and Osborn, 1987). We need, however, to make a more detailed analysis. How would we characterize primary education today? It is clear that there is no such thing as a typical primary school, and that descriptive dichotomies such as traditional-progressive, formal-informal, didactic-discovery are too simplistic.

We do know, however, that, despite the failure of the 'Plowden-approach' to 'revolutionize' many primary schools, they are quite different places from what they were in the days of the eleven-plus. We can identify some generalizable characteristics that seem to be common to primary schools today and would have been uncommon twenty years ago. These are:

● mixed ability classes;

● little overt competition between children;

● a certain informality in the relationship between teacher and child;

● a variety of teaching and learning approaches;

● the integration of some subjects into topic work;

● few 'lessons' in formal subjects, other than maths.

Regular and significant examining in primary schools will, I believe, on the basis of what we know already about the effects of testing, have an impact on each of these characteristics.

The differentiated nature of the assessment will affect classroom organization: since children must be given the level of assessment which suits their ability, decisions will have to be made about levels in advance of the assessment, just as in GCSE, at any rate for the subjects which have differentiated exams (see Gipps et al., 1986). It is likely that children will be given work to suit the level they are at and, as I have already pointed out, grouping according to ability within the classroom will follow. Barker-Lunn suggests that this is already happening (Barker-Lunn, 1984) but differentiation will hasten the trend.

Of course, differentiation is important in that it seems to be the best way of avoiding *redoublement,* the re-taking of a year which has been part of both the French and German systems. At the moment, *redouble-ment* is not envisaged as part of the Secretary of State's plans: it is one aspect of the much-vaunted European system that, presumably, the DES could not accept. Indeed it was abolished in France in the mid-1960s (but continues to operate — so much for the power of central control) and is less popular now in Germany than was the case ten years ago (HMI, 1986). Broadfoot and Osborn (1987) maintain that the fear of *redoublement* for their pupils acts as a stronger constraint on French teachers to follow closely the curriculum objectives laid down than will benchmark tests in the UK. Nevertheless, *redoublement* is a complica-tion we can well do without.

Another corollary of differentiation in particular, and of a formal examining scheme in general, is that it will encourage more overt com-petition among children. This is not to suggest that children in primary schools are not competitive now. They are; they often know who is best at maths or reading. They, and their parents, use whatever evidence comes to hand to make these judgements, whether it is progress through the reading scheme or the number of stars on the tables chart. But this examining system will result in competitiveness of a different kind and degree: the existing competitiveness will be exploited and intensified. For a start, there is the national dimension; scores will be scaled accor-ding to national benchmarks, enabling parents and teachers to evaluate children's progress in relation to some 'national norm'. Indeed the assessment system is specifically designed to enable and encourage this sort of comparison. This will result in competitiveness of a completely different order from that inspired by reading schemes. They will also have a significant material impact on children's experience in terms of grouping (and eventual allocation to type of secondary school), as already pointed out. Children will, therefore, have a great deal more at stake in keeping themselves appraised of their progress in relation to their classmates.

At the moment children can get to the end of primary schooling without ever having failed a test or exam and certainly without feeling they are failures or 'second-rate'. Under the new examining system — the rhetoric of differentiation, which allows every child to show what they can do, aside — this seems most unlikely to continue. More likely are a return to competitiveness and an emphasis on individual effort. But, as Stronach points out (1987), this is precisely what is required by central government. The argument within the White Paper *Working*

Together — *education and training* (DoE, 1986) is that Britain has a serious economic problem because of a lack of competitiveness. People lack motivation and training, therefore: 'motivation is all important so that attitudes change and people acquire the desire to learn, the habit of learning . . .' Thus a return to competitiveness within the primary school is to be encouraged as part of a plan for economic recovery.

Competitiveness is a definite feature of the European system. As Chisholm points out (1987):

> pupils (in Germany) are under great pressure *to achieve* demonstrably and continuously . . . Equally significant is the process of internal socialization in the primary school years, whereby children gradually learn to see grading as personal affirmation.

Children who are able and confident will no doubt flourish in the new system, as in the old, but what about the self-image of the less able children? To encourage them to come to terms with their level of ability at a very much younger age than we currently do means that the real world will enter the world of the primary school. My firm belief is that part of the role of the primary school is to *protect* the young child from the real world while he or she develops at his or her own pace within a secure, supportive environment; this will be much more difficult to achieve within an examination system. Mr. Baker, however, is not concerned about this argument; he is quoted as saying:

> It has become rather unfashionable to give tests to children today because there is the belief that that segregated the winners from the losers . . . parents knew such an approach was bogus (*The Daily Telegraph,* 9 February 1987).

It follows that the teacher will have a different relationship with his or her pupils — not so much that of guide and mentor, but more one based on instruction and assessment. The easy informality which characterizes many primary classrooms must surely become strained as teachers move into a formal assessment role. This change and the re-emergence of more formal relationships may, of course, be popular with many parents who will recognize the formality and discipline of their own school days.

A move towards more didactic teaching styles, and a consequent reduction of other approaches, will be almost inevitable. Research evidence show that if you 'teach' in the traditional manner — imparting knowledge in a structured, controlled way — you can get higher test scores (Bennett, 1987). However, what is often forgotten is the second half of the findings, that there may be gains in the affective domain from informal approaches. What you gain on the swings you lose on the roundabouts — it is a question of which priorities count.

Will there be less time for practical work in the prescribed chunk of time for maths? There was little practical work evident in Germany. What about originality and individuality? HMI asked German primary teachers about this — the response was that they encouraged and accepted originality and individuality but HMI could see little evidence of either in the children's written work (HMI, 1986, p.17).

The future of integrated topic work will also be under question. The consultation document says that the working parties in some subject areas may need to have primary specialists:

> For some subject areas, such as history and geography, or the expressive subjects including art and music, a special group or sub-group to cover integrated studies in the primary phase may be needed. Likewise a sub-group to pull together work on science and technology in the primary phase may be appropriate (DES, 1987, p.26).

This sounds extremely tentative, but we could be optimistic and hope for the best. Certainly, since English, maths and science — the three core subjects — are to have separate assessments and programmes of work, they are clearly unlikely to be integrated aspects of the curriculum. We shall, therefore, see a return to more formally-bounded subjects and subject lessons.

Finally, given the way in which I have described current primary schooling — albeit in general terms — it is clear that, for many primary school children, being examined or tested is going to be a stressful experience, even if it is handled informally and sensitively. We know that this is the case already even with one-off group reading tests; and Margaret Brown and her colleagues have recently found the same with group administered diagnostic tests in maths (Denvir and Brown, 1987).

What then of the positive impact of the proposed national curriculum, and of its examinations, for primary schools? There must, after all, be some implications that we can regard as beneficial. There are three which immediately spring to mind. First, there must be an increase in science teaching since 'the majority of curriculum time at primary level should be devoted to the core subjects' (i.e. English, maths and science) (DES, 1987, p.6). But still no foreign language!

Second, following on from differentiation we may see a better match between level of task and the child's ability to do it. This is currently a serious weakness in the quality of primary teaching (see Bennett et al., 1984).

Third, parents should be better informed about what their children are doing, can do and how they compare with classmates. Most parents are passionately interested in these questions, and it has been a failure of much modern primary work — despite parental involvement in the early stages of schooling — to explain to parents what their children are doing and why.

Another possibly beneficial outcome goes something like this: at the moment primary teachers have rather vague but all-encompassing objectives which involve supporting the all-round development of the child; as a consequence they find it hard to achieve these and blame themselves for not delivering the goods rather than questioning the objectives. 'After all . . . all children would and could develop correctly if only teachers were good enough' (Walkerdine, 1984). Broadfoot and Osborn suggest (1987) that French teachers who have narrower objectives — their main one being to avoid *redoublement* for their pupils — are more likely than their English colleagues to feel satisfied that they have achieved them. So, it may be that in the 1990s when primary teachers have got used to the idea of the national curriculum, regular exams and assessments, and to being technicians delivering an unproblematic and fixed curriculum, that they will get satisfaction from achieving their objectives, that is, getting an acceptable number of children to pass their exams. You never can tell.

* * *

To conclude, my view is that the disadvantages associated with the proposed system of national assessment at primary level outweigh the possible positive impact. Primary schools under the new arrangements will be a good deal more like secondary schools in being under the influence of exam board constraints. More ability banding, more competition, formal teaching relationships and methods, stricter subject boundaries: these are the familiar artefacts of public exams in secondary schools. Is this what we want for primary education? For this is what exams would mean.

Acknowledgement

My thanks are due to Barry Stierer who commented on an earlier verson of this paper.

References

Armstrong, M. (1987), 'Bench-marks', *The Times Educational Supplement,* 15 May.

Barker-Lunn, J. (1984), 'Junior school teachers; their methods and practices', *Educational Research,* pp.178-87.

Bennett, N., Desforges, C., Cockburn, A. and Wilkinson, B. (1984), *The Quality of Pupil Learning Experiences.* Lawrence Erlbaum Associates.

Bennett, N. (1987), 'Changing perspectives on teaching-learning processes in the post-Plowden era', *Oxford Review of Education,* Vol.13, No.1.

Broadfoot, P. and Osborn, M. (1987), 'French lessons', *The Times Educational Supplement,* 3 July.

Chisholm, L. (1987), 'Vorsprung ex machina? Aspects of curriculum and assessment in cultural comparison', *Journal of Education Policy,* Vol.2, No.2, pp.149-59.

Denvir, B. and Brown, M. (1987), 'The feasibility of class-administered diagnostic assessment in primary maths', *Educational Research,* Vol.29, No.2.

Department of Education and Science (1987), *The National Curriculum 5-16: a consultation document.* London: DES, July.

Department of Employment (1986), *Working Together — education and training*. White Paper, Cmnd 9823. London: HMSO.

Gipps, C., Steadman, S., Blackstone, T. and Stierer, B. (1983), *Testing Children; standardized testing in schools and LEAs*. London: Heinemann Educational Books.

Gipps, C. (ed.) (1986), *The GCSE: an uncommon examination*. Bedford Way Paper No. 29. London: Institute of Education, University of London.

Gipps, C., Gross, H. and Goldstein, H. (1987), *Warnock's 18 per-cent: children with special needs in the primary school*. Basingstoke: Falmer Press.

Her Majesty's Inspectorate (1986), *Education in the Federal Republic of Germany: aspects of curriculum and assessment*. London: HMSO.

Lawton, D. (1987), 'Cutting the curriculum cloth', *The Times Educational Supplement,* 1 May.

Rosenthal, R. and Jacobson, L. (1968), *Pygmalion in the Classroom: teacher expectation and pupils' intellectual development*. New York, London: Holt, Reinhart and Winston.

Stronach, I. (1987), 'Ten years on', *Forum,* Vol.29, No.3, summer.

Walkerdine, V. (1984), 'Developmental psychology and the child-centred pedagogy', in J. Henriques et al., *Changing the Subject*. London: Methuen.

Teacher Professionalism and the National Curriculum

Helen Simons

In the plethora of critique that has accompanied the National Curriculum consultation document, relatively little attention has been paid to the professional role of the teacher and the loss to our education system of the pedagogical and curriculum developments that have taken place over the past twenty-five years.

Let me make my position clear at the outset. I am committed to the notion that self-direction by accountable professionals offers the best hope of continuous improvement in the educational experience offered to children by schools. This is not a blind belief but rather, as I hope to demonstrate, one grounded in experience and backed by evidence.

The concept of self-direction, though it seems to some like teacher protectionism, does not entail insulation against lay influences on what professionals do, or lay judgement of how well they do it. On the contrary, it presumes a service orientation, and commitment to mediating a community brief in terms of the educational needs of particular children. This minimal definition of professionalism may, as I shall argue, not be entirely foreclosed to teachers by the proposed national curriculum and assessment system. It is too early to say. But the kind of professionalism to which a growing number of teachers now aspires means much more than this.

The professionals I have in mind evaluate what they do against self-generated critical standards, they research shortfalls in provision and performance, they respond to changes of context or clientele, they experiment, they reflect, they develop new programmes to solve identified problems, they collaborate, they engage in persuasive negotiation with the constituencies whose support and approval they need, (see: House and Lapan, 1987; Hoyle,1975; Stenhouse, 1975; Wise et al., 1984; for other definitions). This kind of teacher professionalism, whose nurture has been the most striking and innovative feature of in-service education over the past fifteen years, will be stopped in its tracks by the current legislation.,

The implication in the National Curriculum consultation document (DES, 1987a, paragraph 51) is that there will be no room for curriculum development other than that related to the national curriculum and only then by schools chosen by the Secretary of State. Clause Nine in the Education Reform Bill reinforces this point and strengthens the powers of the Secretary of State further. While it does not exclude LEAs and governing bodies from applying to become experimental schools, regular reporting to the Secretary of State is required. He even has the power to revoke an earlier decision. Thus 'freedom' to experiment is at the whim of the Secretary of State, a situation deplored by Sheila Browne, former Chief Inspector of HMI, in her speech in January 1988 to the North of England Conference on Education (Browne, 1988). At a stroke, any opportunity for curriculum development outside government control is swept away. When Stuart Maclure told the School Curriculum Development Conference in Leeds in September 1987 that 'there is a great deal to play for' (O'Connor, 1987, p.42), clearly it was not this he had in mind.

In this chapter I shall set out why I believe this outcome of the legislation constitutes both an appalling waste of human talent and an elimination of the only credible option left to us if we are serious about improving standards in schools. But let me begin with a more general view of the role of education professionals in the context of current proposals.

Implementing the National Plan — the use and abuse of professionalism

This is a testing time for the Government. The personal success of the Prime Minister has enabled her to establish a power elite in command of her majority as the basis for radical reform of the welfare state. The power of this elite has recently been put to the test of professional and public opposition with regard to the health service. That particular contest, at the time of writing, seems finely balanced, with the Government locked in battle with the gods of the medical world, the formerly all-powerful consultants, now feeling the draught as the nurses vote with their feet. No one could at this point predict the outcome with confidence.

Can we say the same of schooling, now at the centre of legislative action? Here the issues are less clear-cut, the public interest more differentiated, the scope for deterrence less certain. Whereas health is seen as a life or death issue, schooling is merely a better or worse issue. Closing schools is not the same as closing wards. Nobody queues for education. Quality of provision, and equality of opportunity, constitute the kernel of the education debate. And we have no gods, nor uncontested claim to the kind of Florence Nightingale imagery that nurses enjoy.

And yet, and yet. The warm endorsement by Mr. Baker of the Report of the Task Group on Assessment and Testing (DES, 1987b), a report which fundamentally rejects the ideology of the power elite in almost every respect, reveals a dilemma at the heart of the Government's Reform Bill, as well as confirming Mr. Baker's unstated but increasingly obvious discomfiture with the task Mrs. Thatcher has set him. This dilemma is absent from the health service debate. No one questions the centrality of professional expertise, professional skills, and professional judgements in the determination of patient treatment. The argument is about funding, efficiency, accountability and choice.

In the matter of schooling, on the other hand, the professional determination of pupil treatment is a major target of the Government attack. Should the Bill be enacted and implemented in its present form, the national curriculum will take the place of local professional judgement of common provision, testing and schemes of work will confine pedagogy to what is conducive to publicly comparable performance, and the responsibility for curriculum experimentation, development, growth and change — the hallmark of educational professionalism — will no longer be the concern of teachers, schools or localities. They are destined to become the implementers of curricula, judged nevertheless by the success of treatments they no longer devise.

The dilemma is this: the Government cannot design and build the new state monopoly without the active collaboration of professional educators, because the task of simplifying, standardizing and monitoring the curriculum is a task that calls for sophisticated professional skills. Mr. Baker needs the Paul Blacks of the education world to generate the means, and all the curriculum specialists to generate the schemes of work and the benchmarks of achievement. If the 'providers' and the 'consumers' are to replace the 'producers' in charge of education, he needs a lot of first-class producers to conspire in the take-over. Such individuals are not (give or take a few) technicians for hire. They are professionals with a professional constituency to answer to. They have an interest in better schooling, and a view of how it might be accomplished. That view, seasoned and matured in many cases by the experience of post-war curriculum reform initiatives, is not, in general, in accord with Government convictions. In particular, as the Black Report offers early indication, the professional view of those outside the classroom tends to see enhanced teacher professionalism within it as the cornerstone of improved standards of service. This is reflected, too, in the volume of professional criticism directed at the Government's unbelievably antiquated curriculum thinking, and in public ambivalence at the prospect of a supermarket of schools under consumer management. Although few people enthuse about the quality of the schooling their children receive, not many are convinced that the Government and the consumer can do a better job of it.

In the coming months of legislative process, and the subsequent years of laborious and protracted enactment, education professionals will continue to engage the simplistic nostrums of policy and attempt to convert them into constructive proposals. Many related and associated issues will of course be resolved soon, one way or the other, issues that are exclusively matters of legislation — the redistribution of formal powers, the introduction of new rights. These are rightly the issues that currently command the headlines — opting out, open enrolment, resourcing, school management — the framing legislation within which the new curriculum and assessment system will be constructed.

But that system will not spring full-fleshed from a parliamentary decision. It will have to be constructed piece by piece, stage by stage, over a lengthy period of time. And it is during that process, which looks as if it might take ten years, that the basic conditions of teachers' work will gradually emerge. That is a long time, it is strewn with uncertainties, and there is still a lot to gain or lose.

The Government has made its vision of better schooling perfectly clear. The professionals have made their opposition clear, but not their alternative vision. It is to that alternative vision that this chapter is addressed, in the belief that, though the legislative battle may be lost, the curriculum war is just beginning.

* * *

'The full force of teachers' professionalism will need to be put behind the national curriculum and assessment if both are to be beneficial to pupils and other "customers" of the education service' (DES, 1987a, paragraph 67). How true, and how unlikely, in view of the fact that the preceding sixty-six paragraphs describe a curriculum improvement strategy — the teacher-proof packaged curriculum, that was tested to destruction in the first wave of post-war curriculum reform. Here it is again, the old centre-periphery model, now reinforced with statutory concrete, ready for the relaunch. The appeal to teacher professionalism in such a context has a distinctly hollow ring.

Yet teacher professionalism, ironically, is at the heart of the alternative vision to which I referred, and by-pass strategies no longer command the confidence that was once invested in them. Twenty-five years of sustained and systematic effort to improve the educational quality of schooling, especially the quality of secondary schooling for all, have generated, cumulatively and often painfully, a body of experienced-based learning about the limitations of social engineering and some promising alternative paths to improvement. This learning is notable by its complete absence from Government thinking.

Twenty-five years of curriculum review, innovation, and development have also taught us another lesson that the Government chooses to ignore, and that many critical commentators seem to have overlooked. This is that 'breadth and balance', so regularly intoned by ministers in justification of the foundation curriculum, is far less a function of subject structure than it is of how individual subjects are conceived and taught. This notion of breadth and balance is partly, I suspect, what Mr. Baker sees as 'clutter'. It is found where you find good teachers, and it is not incompatible with a national curriculum. It is however, fatally undermined by subjection to conventional achievement tests, which depend upon narrowly stipulative domains of learning.

Learning from the past

In her speech to the School Curriculum Development Committee's National Conference in September, 1987, the Minister of State for Education, Angela Rumbold, acknowledged that 'an enormous amount of curriculum development work has taken place in the schools, in education departments in universities and within LEAs and, of course, not least, most recently through the School Curriculum Development Committee'. 'So we are not starting from scratch,' she went on to say, 'nor abandoning all the very good work that has been done' (O'Connor, 1987, p.29). The remainder of her speech showed little awareness of what that curriculum development work entailed nor how it could be built upon. It may be useful to remind ourselves, as well as inform Mrs. Rumbold, of some of those developments.

Anyone with enough power can change schools for the worse. How to change them for the better is the problem, a problem that has preoccupied the industralized democracies increasingly since the end of the Second World War. In the USA, the first to convert preoccupation into intervention, the priority was seen to be curriculum modernization with particular attention to the 'fast track' students. University-based star academics led the change, producing glossy new textbooks for supposedly star-struck teachers. It was thought to be as simple as that, especially since the initiative had been preceded by a ferocious and concerted attack on the incompetence and complacency of American teachers.

By the time American attention had shifted, in the Kennedy era, from elite reinforcement to compensatory education for the poor, low achieving, discriminated against and increasingly politicized minorities, a more compound view of the problem of improving schools had risen from the ashes of initial naivety. The nicely-wrapped, expertly constructed teacher-proof packages had wrought little by way of change in intended learning outcomes. Maybe R D and D (Research, Development and Diffusion), the basic elements and stages of the centre-periphery model, required further thought and refinement. Maybe independent evaluation (mandated in 1965) could ensure that federal funds reached their destination, that problems of implementation were looked at, that feedback was received.

One or two voices suggested that teachers might be important, and that the strategy of softening them up to weaken their resistance to change was poor psychology if they were. But it was not really until the mid-1980s that teachers — their thinking, their training, their development as key agents in the effort to improve schooling — moved to centre stage in curriculum reform theory. And by that time, an analytic review of twenty years of federal intervention in the cause of improvement (Atkin and House, 1981) had concluded that the money might as well have been distributed directly to schools. Not altogether

bad news for Washington, since federal involvement was in any case
in the process of retreat and curtailment, faced down by State resent-
ment at federal meddling in their affairs.

Have the American schools improved? Some say yes: to some extent
the disadvantaged have gained more access, and more opportunities
to compete and succeed through cafeteria-style options and credits.
Others, certainly the vocal majority, point to the continuing decline
evidenced in test scores. Many of those who can afford it are 'opting
out' of the public schools and 'going private'. The Neo-Conservatives
want a set menu to replace the cafeteria, perhaps a foundation curriculum. Sounds familiar? Mr. Baker, on a recent visit to the USA,
must have displayed a remarkable gift for evenhandedness about the
issue, publicly extolling the superior qualities of the American public
school whilst, presumably, and privately, endorsing the proposals of
its most scathing denigrators.

In this country we have come to the same arguments, but by a different route. In one sense, the story is the inverse of the American one.
Beginning with the Nuffield projects and ending with the national curriculum, the tale is one of the gradual marginalization of the teacher
from an initial position of centrality in the generation of national
initiatives, and the gradual accretion of state control, first by the
bureaucracy but ultimately by the ruling political elite.

It was classroom teachers, members of the Association for Science
Education, who persuaded the Nuffield Foundation to back their ideas
for revamping the content and pedagogy of secondary school science.

It was teachers who won control of the Schools Council when that
ill-fated political compromise took over the Nuffield mantle with a more
comprehensive responsibility for curriculum development. It was mainly
teachers on secondment from classrooms who staffed the numerous
national curriculum development projects spawned by the Council in
the 1960s, when faith in the transformative capacity of such endeavours
was at its height, and teachers in the pilot schools tested, and in some
cases refined and redesigned, the centrally produced packages.

Yes, it was the package philosophy again, the centre-periphery
assumptions again. The same results again? Many thought so, especially
those would-be but marginalized interventionists stamping their feet
impatiently in the corridors of Whitehall. Certainly there was no instant
transformation, no stampede of RSLA (Raising of the School Leaving
Age) teacher consumers to the supermarket of curriculum merchandise

created by the Council. The Government saw its chance, attacked the Council's record, mortally undermined it, decided to abolish it, and then for good measure commissioned a virtually posthumous evaluation.

When the reaction set in, we were well into the 1970s, into the recession, managerialism, and into a new centre-periphery model, less civilized than its predecessor, less liberal in its educational pretensions, more assertive in pursuing its categorical targets in a school system beginning to feel the chill of resource reduction. Systems thinking, the epitome of rational design for social engineers, was the new byword for effective action. The language changed, but not to that of the Renaissance civil servants in charge. Now it was the task force, not the team, objectives rather than aims, managers rather than leaders, steering rather than consultative committees. The language of support and choice, the soft-sell of the 1960s, changed in the 1970s to the language of the hard-sell, the language of power.

There is no evidence that these power-coercive tendencies were any more effective than the friendly persuasion that preceded them, and much to be said for the view that their greater precision gave them less purchase on the relevant variables. But power, once taken, was never likely to be relinquished, and as educational change moved inexorably up the scale of the political agenda, becoming in the end the object of competitive bidding between aspiring politicians, the internal logic of developments led us to Mr. Baker's 'final solution'.

What happened to the teachers? That's another story, and a different learning curve. Some went back to school, but many developed new and unexpected careers, moving into the new occupational space created by the curriculum reform movement — as local education authority advisers, as teacher centre leaders, as HMIs, as teacher educators, as polytechnic and university-based specialists in the various dimensions of curriculum change processes. They constituted a new breed of curriculum professionals, and they quickly began, in collaboration with many incumbents who had observed and absorbed the experience of curriculum innovation from the sidelines, to change the face of educational studies, of in-service courses, and of research into education.

Like the Government, these professionals drew conclusions from their experience of the difficulties of securing significant change in teaching practice. But they drew different conclusions and developed different advocacies and practices, advocacies and practices which were increasingly at odds with Government inclinations. Let me try to encapsulate some of the conclusions which are of most relevance to the theme of this chapter.

First, an early conviction. There can be no curriculum development without teacher development. The package philosophy is a red herring. The involvement of teachers in a generative role in curriculum determination is essential to good practice. Teachers make poor operatives of other people's ideas.

Next, an associated conviction. Teachers cannot break through to and sustain new practice without support at the institutional and local advisory level. Obvious now perhaps, but many curriculum projects had assumed they could work directly and exclusively with individual classroom teachers. Change is a professional community activity.

Then, a more general observation on the locus of decision-making. No two schools are so alike in their circumstances (history, resources, clienteles) for prescriptions of curricular action to adequately supplant the judgements of those who work in them.

Next, and sometime later, a more daunting conclusion. There can be no significant teacher development, and therefore no curriculum change, without institutional change. Institutional values act to frustrate, limit and neutralize individual teacher development.

Finally, the whole recipe for policy and action. Neither the free market (the rationale of curriculum development in the 1960s) nor command/compliance (the rationale more characteristic of the 1970s and 1980s) appear to yield the quality of curriculum change that is sought. We should think, rather, in terms of educational communities of professionals and their constituencies, working together in a spirit of shared responsibility and mutual accountability.

These were, and remain, the foundation stones of the alternative vision to which I referred earlier in the chapter — decentralized curriculum decision-making, local accountability, institutional change, teacher-generated development — and all of these crucially dependent upon the energizing force of a concept of fully-fledged teacher professionalism.

The growth of professionalism

The vision inspired a movement that has gathered momentum over the past twenty years. Its origins are commonly traced to Lawrence

Stenhouse's advocacy of the 'teacher as researcher', a notion embodied in the Humanities Curriculum Project, which invited teachers to research a problem of curricular action rather than offer them curriculum prescriptions. The notion inspired subsequent projects such as the Ford Teaching Project and NARTAR, (National Association for Race Relations Teaching and Action Research) which established national and regional networks of teachers committed to researching their practice. Subject associations like NATE (National Association for the Teaching of English) and LATE (London Association for the Teaching of English) for example, were also prominent in developing networks of teachers devoted to improving their teaching. Those responsible for in-service education began to provide the crucial support necessary to sustain such innovative developments.

In-service efforts went beyond the process of curriculum renewal to generating courses for teacher development. The concept of the teacher embedded in many of these courses was clearly that of the professional or the extended professional. Teacher researcher networks spread rapidly. The Curriculum Action Research network, perhaps the most well-known, now has links in the United States, Australia, Iceland, Austria, Spain and many other European countries as well. During this period, universities and colleges of education were increasingly engaging their students in researching their own work as part of their teacher education. This undoubtedly helped to strengthen and extend a grass-roots movement concerned to extend the professionalism of teachers.

When in the mid-1970s it became clear that teacher development was also dependent upon institutional development (Simons, 1987), more opportunities arose for teachers collectively to develop their professional skills. The school self-evaluation movement took account of both one of the major deficiencies of the curriculum project reform movement — the failure effectively to match curriculum programmes to the culture of individual schools — and one of the deficiencies of the teacher development movement — the failure effectively to link the work of individual teachers on off-site courses with on-site development work in schools.

The introduction of TVEI, GCSE and GRIST developments have all accelerated the professional development of teachers in a number of interesting but different ways. The introduction of TVEI is an imaginative variation of centre-periphery thinking in which central guidelines are combined with teacher creativity in the interpretation of a brief. This freedom has in some circumstances enabled teachers to promote liberal values within a vocationally-oriented government priority and to adopt many of the inquiry-based approaches to learning that have developed over the past twenty years (Pring, 1987). Staff development, inter-institutional collaboration and related in-service support have also been features of TVEI provision.

GCSE preparations have been of a different order, focusing upon the specifics of inducting teachers into the range of different assessment procedures the new examination demands. These and the pedagogical implications of some of the new procedures call for sophisticated professional skills on the part of teachers.

GRIST arrangements hold promise for facilitating further professional development of teachers, schools and local education authorities. Many LEAs are already experimenting with ways of integrating institutional development plans with local education authority plans and national priorities and with different ways of allocating resources to different groups within the authority to facilitate professional development of staff at all levels — school, adviser, officer.

There are many other developments I could mention that have built upon the growth of professionalism at classroom and school level. The Kettering Alternative Approach in Northamptonshire (Simons et al., 1987), for instance, a joint curriculum development exercise across six schools to improve learning opportunities across the town, has already shown how collaborative educational communities may be initiated and organized.

This movement, which has steadily gathered strength and membership since it was initiated in the early 1970s, still looks the most promising of all post-war reform initiatives concerned to improve the quality of schooling. It is the product of a professional distillation of all we have learned about curriculum development. It is about to be trampled underfoot.

Concluding comments

One remains baffled by the national curriculum and what it represents. It is hardly the embodiment of free-market philosophy. It holds no particular promise in terms of economic manpower requirements. Indeed, it appears to stand on its head the previous policies of this administration. It offers little to consumers in search of choice of provision. Is it merely the arbitrary scaffolding of a test programme that will facilitate the occupational credentialling of the Tory electorate? Is it simply the logical outcome of the accretion of political power? Is it a way of keeping education out of schooling? Is it a subtle (too subtle for me) way of minimizing future costs? Is it really a defence against left-wing local councils? I wish I knew, because then we would know that one of its major consequences may be unintended — a demoralizing demotion of teachers and the virtual extinction of creativity in curricular action.

If this is indeed an unintended consequence, then there is some hope that the coming years of close involvement of education professionals in the process of constructing its substantial form will salvage and keep alive the prospect of professional life for teachers. Paul Black has made a promising start, but Mrs. Thatcher is reportedly displeased, and apparently not for turning. The loss, in that case, will be enormous. Not just the termination of a promising movement to extend and enhance teacher professionalism, but a certain erosion of the levels of teacher commitment we can readily lay claim to, and that are widely acknowledged by other countries.

Without the opportunity to contribute to the formulation of aims, processes and the kind of educational experiences likely to realize them, without the opportunity to teach creatively, not simply to the prescriptions of others, and without the support necessary to sustain personal growth, the level of professionalism in the system is certain to decline and with it the quality of education. The national curriculum, in this sense and within this perspective, is a folly of unprecedented proportions.

References

Atkin, J.M. and House, E.R. (1981), 'The federal role in curriculum development, 1950-80', *Educational Evaluation and Policy Analysis,* Vol.3, No.5, pp.5-36.

Browne, S. (1988), Presidential Address to the North of England Conference on Education: 'In search of excellence', January 4-6. Reported in *Education,* 8 January 1988.

Department of Education and Science (1987a), *The National Curriculum 5-16: a consultation document.* London: DES, July.

Department of Education and Science (1987b), *National Curriculum: Task Group on Assessment and Testing: a report*. London: DES, December.

Elliott, J. (1976), *Developing Hypotheses about Classrooms from Teachers' Practical Constructs*. An account of the work of the Ford Teaching Project, North Dakota Study Group on Evaluation. Grand Forks: University of North Dakota Press, in association with the Cambridge Institute of Education.

Elliott, J. and Adelman, C. (1976), 'Innovation at the classroom level: case study of the Ford Teaching Project', *Curriculum Design and Development,* Course E203, Unit 28. Milton Keynes: Open University Press, pp.52-64.

House, E. and Lapan, S. (1987), 'Teacher appraisal', in J. Elliott, and H. Simons, (1988) *Rethinking Assessment and Appraisal*. Milton Keynes: Open University Press.

Hoyle, E.W. (1975), 'The creativity of the school in Britain', in A. Harris, M. Lawn, and W. Prescott (eds.), *Curriculum Innovation*. London: Croom Helm in association with the Open University Press.

O'Connor, M. (1987), *Curriculum at the Crossroads:* an account of the SCDC national conference 'Aspects of Curriculum Change', University of Leeds, September 1987. London: School Curriculum Development Committee.

Pring R. (1987), 'No lessons learnt from TVEI', in M. Golby, *Perspectives on the National Curriculum,* Perspectives 32, School of Education, University of Exeter.

Simons, H. (1987), *Getting to Know Schools in a Democracy: the politics and process of evaluation*. Basingstoke: Falmer Press.

Simons, H., Elliott, J. and MacDonald, B. (1987), *Kettering Alternative Approach: independent external evaluation report on the second year, 1986-1987*.

Stenhouse, L. (1975), *An Introduction to Curriculum Research and Development*. London: Heinemann.

Wise, A.E., Darling-Hammond, L., McLaughlin, M. and Bernstein, H. (1984), *Teacher Evaluation: a study of effective practices*. The Rand Corporation for the National Institute of Education, June.

Running up the Down Escalator: crisis management as curriculum management

Janet Harland

It is quite possible that government is trying to extend its control over the education system and to impose a national curriculum not because it is becoming *more* competent and ambitious to control, *more* keen to implement macro-solutions to pressing problems and *more* certain that it has the right, the know-how and the electorate's confidence in its efforts, but precisely because it is none of these things.

Commentary on recent developments in education policy in Britain has tended to move very speedily from description to Jeremiah-like expressions of woe. Steering well clear of drawing parallels with other areas of social and economic policy, many writers have described educational and curriculum policy-making in terms of a purposive thrust towards centralization. By and large this is explained either as a careful campaign to install an educational ideology consistent with the broader policies of the party in power or, alternatively, as a more or less inevitable consequence of the development of modern management strategies and pervasive bureaucratic controls. There is, however, another way of looking at events since the middle 1970s, to which the emergence of a national curriculum appears as a logical conclusion. This involves using the idea of 'legitimation crisis', a crisis which, it is said, has come to structure the actions of government in Western industrialized countries. Such ideas are derived from neo-Marxist theories of state and are most fully developed in the work of Jurgen Habermas.

* * *

The appeal of such a theory relates to the fact that it appears to address the enormity of the task which confronts modern governments. It is argued that in most industrialized countries, the state has effectively replaced the market as the steering mechanism of capitalist systems. Government now assumes responsibility for the quality of life, for the welfare of citizens and hence for the maintenance of the economy in a state sufficiently prosperous to meet the minimum demands and expectations of its citizenry. Writers such as Habermas and Claus Offe have demonstrated the virtually insoluble tension for advanced capitalist societies between creating the conditions for capital accumulation and simultaneously ensuring a level of redistribution of wealth which satisfies the populace. Indeed, 'all such societies must resolve the problem of distributing surplus social product inequitably but legitimately' (Habermas, 1975). The economic policies of our present Government are an eloquent testimony to this tension.

Not only do governments have to contend with these problems but they have to do so in a world in which there is an increasing erosion of public confidence in the state's capacity to meet its obligations. Hence the idea that there is a state of crisis concerning the 'legitimacy' of governmental attempts to steer their systems: as the public perceives what would appear to be increasing levels of failure in relation to the whole spectrum of social and economic policy, it starts to question not only the capacity of the centre but even its basic right to institute corrective policies. 'Legitimacy means that there are good arguments for a political order's claim to be recognized as right and just' (Habermas, 1979, quoted in Wuthnow et al., 1984); yet when government fails to deliver the goods (whether in relation to employment, health care, housing, education, or countless other areas of public concern) both right and justice are queried. Faced with such a situation, the state is driven to find new strategies and new arguments with which to bolster its weakening claims; and yet the irony is that such attempts are likely, on this thesis, to create a new set of disjunctions between the perceived task of government and its capacity to fulfil that task.

The move towards greater control of the curriculum might therefore be seen as little more than a knee-jerk response to crisis. Put simply, the less we believe parliamentary government capable of resolving our educational problems, the more politicians charged with running an increasingly discredited system will seek new ways to demonstrate the legitimacy of their policies. They will find that they need to promise more and hence to control more; but the chances of success may well be slim.

*   *   *

In this chapter, I propose to look at various strategies by which government is seeking to legitimate its right to determine educational programmes. In doing this I shall refer to a recent paper on a similar theme by Hans Weiler concerning the West German education system, so often held up as a model of how things should be done: I shall endeavour to demonstrate that despite the considerable differences in the *content* of education policy between the two countries, there are significant parallels in the attempts to legitimize those interventions. I shall then briefly explore the links between legitimation (justification?) and enforcement (the effort to ensure that policies devised — and hopefully legitimated — at the centre are actually implemented at the periphery). As in the Peter Wright-*Spycatcher* case, the crucial question is whether the law is an ass because it is unenforceable. If that should be the case, what credibility could the legitimation process have?

Following mainstream legitimation arguments, Weiler claims that in making and implementing educational policy, the state has to deal with a 'dual crisis' relating both to the structural problems of advanced capitalism and to a crisis of confidence in the public education system. He suggests that, faced with the need to recapture its position, the West German government has embarked upon a three-pronged strategy of 'compensatory legitimation': namely

(a) The 'legalization' or 'judicialization' of educational policy, primarily reflected in the increased role of the courts in educational policy;

(b) the utilization of expertise in the policy-making process, especially through such devices as experimentation and planning;

(c) the development and stipulation of participatory forms of decision-making in education (Weiler, 1983).

Over the past decade, German opinion has been increasingly concerned about the ever closer relationship between education and the law, notably through the increase in the number of legal specifications within administrative regulations; the increase in the number of court cases; the growing use of legal argument in public debate about education; and (most significantly as far as present parallels with Britain are concerned) 'the increased role of parliamentary legislation as a source of educational norms' (ibid.). The issues which are most commonly the focus of such legalization are identified as curriculum, differentiation and the rights of minority groups. What was previously considered to be adequately dealt with within the system, by administrative decision or within the normal exercise of professional judgement, is now seen as an appropriate object of formal legislative action, democratic rights thus being endorsed by democratically legitimated action. Weiler suggests that such legalizing processes may be more necessary for policies devised by Federal rather than local government, for at the more remote level problems of legitimacy may be more pressing. However, he also points to increasing public scepticism about parliamentary representative processes and argues that the function of the courts may be to bolster the effectiveness and acceptability of central law-making.

In this country we have given less attention to increasing legalization; yet it is a useful way in which to view the changes of the past decade. From exhortation and selective financial inducement, government has turned increasingly to legislation to bring about changes in education. With Education Bills in 1980, 1981, 1986, and the biggest of them all in 1987, wider and wider areas of school practice are now being specifically framed by law. Parental choice of schools, the provision for pupils with special needs, the publication of brochures and of examination results, the constitution and responsibilities of governing bodies, even teaching about sex and politics: all these are now determined by national political processes and no longer by local professional and bureaucratic practices. The curriculum itself will be enshrined in statutory law. The range of subjects, the balance between them, and the processes of testing pupils and monitoring schools to ensure compliance will all be determined by our elected government, no doubt loudly claiming a mandate for each and every detail of the package; for the legitimacy of such intervention is based on an appeal to the democratic process of legislation.

Some would say that the British are fortunate in that education has only rarely been the subject of legal dispute in the courts. Aggrieved persons have mostly sought redress by appealing to local and, beyond them, national officials or elected representatives. However, it seems more than likely that parents and others may in future pursue in the courts opportunities which are apparently promised by legislation and yet appear to have been denied to them. If my child's school refuses to teach her a foreign language to sixteen or proposes too 'soft' an interpretation of what constitutes genuine technology, or if the local authority fails to provide an adequate supply of qualified teachers and suitable resources to deliver the promised curriculum, surely litigation will be the obvious resort? Parallel to this, we are likely to see a marked increase in the use of legal arguments from different levels in the system in comments on the capacity or willingness of others to meet their statutory obligations. Already we can note the rapid increase in apparently legally binding arrangements of all kinds within the education system. Most notably, the Manpower Services Commission has introduced the notion of 'contract' into its negotiations with providers of education and training; the Technical and Vocational Education Initiative is the clearest but not the only example, and there is evidence that the Department of Education and Science is increasingly favouring similar arrangements in the context of schemes funded by specific grant.

Thus we can see in Britain also a steady increase in the legalization and judicialization of the system despite the many problems that such a trend implies. Tim Brighouse has recently pointed out (Brighouse, 1987) that much of the legislation is mutually contradictory, with the proposals for 1987 undermining what was enacted in 1980, 1981 and 1986; for example, the obligation to publish test results for all age levels coupled with the increased right for parents to opt for the school of their choice, regardless of LEA attempts to regulate numbers, will militate against attempts to integrate children with special needs into mainstream schools. Again, there are many manifest anomalies in relation to the curriculum of independent schools, city technology colleges, grant-maintained schools and the residue. However, my argument is that this lack of inherent logic is neither surprising nor particularly relevant. The resort to legislation is best understood as an attempt to assert the right and the effectiveness of the state as regulator of the education system in the face of increasing public criticism.

* * *

The second strategy identified by Weiler refers to legitimation by expertise, and in particular by experimentation. One example that he draws from West Germany is the attempt in the late 1960s and early 1970s to evaluate different forms of post-elementary schooling on a comparative basis.

The need for the state to discover new forms of legitimation in the 'imperatives of scientific-technical progress' (Wilby, 1979) is a central theme of the Habermas thesis. 'The only problems are technical problems and the development of the social system must obey the logic of scientific progress' (ibid.). The appeal of the experiment is therefore obvious. In Britain there has been less explicit 'experimentation' on the agricultural-botanical model but there has been an increasing dependence on the pilot project, particularly in relation to curriculum and assessment. Major examples are the Technical and Vocational Education Initiative, the Lower Attaining Pupils Project, the Records of Achievement pilot schemes and the current DES-sponsored experiments with teacher appraisal. These schemes are far from open-ended explorations. TVEI, for example, was massively extended before its outcomes could be properly evaluated; and of the others it is possible to say that the only apparently unresolved questions are about implementation, the zero option being simply not available. However, the very existence of pilots enables government to claim a deference to the lessons of trial and error and to the 'expertise' thus generated.

Habermas claims that the search for technically-expert solutions allows more and more social questions to be taken out of the realm of public debate — which leads to the depoliticization of the masses. (This, despite the fact that increasingly interventionist legislation brings the state further and further into the regulation of everyday life.) Certainly Weiler suggests that one virtue of experimentation is that it suspends conflict by 'seemingly constructive temporizing'. Either way, it appears to diminish the scope for arguments based on value and principle by demonstrating that policy emerges from rational enquiry and objective fact. Such strategies have clearly played their part in the formulation of plans for a national curriculum and its various adjuncts such as teacher appraisal. Government has involved the teachers, the researchers, the academics, the industrialists in pilot schemes, and it has apparently demonstrated a commitment to reform. So it appears that reason itself, rather than political ideology, dictates that we must now go forward.

*   *   *

Weiler's third strategy relates to public participation:

> The basic argument is that the state, faced with an erosion of legitimacy which stems in no small part from the particular credibility problems of systems of representation, attempts to re-generate the basis of its own legitimation by tolerating or actually setting up schemes for client involvement or citizen participation (Weiler, 1983).

Weiler goes on to argue that curricular decisions are inherently conflictual in that there can be no final decision on whether the interests of the individual or those of the state should predominate. Thus decisions on the curriculum immediately raise the question of the state's right to determine issues on which there are apparently irresolvable disagreements and therefore such decisions have 'extraordinarily high legitimation needs'. Accordingly, attempts to meet such needs 'derive added credibility and legitimacy from the participation of those affected by the outcomes of the decision process'.

Since 1976 the Government in Britain has endeavoured to increase public participation in curriculum matters. However, unlike Germany where the emphasis has been largely on encouraging teacher participation in designing the details of curriculum packages, the intention here has been largely to widen the constituency, notably by including parents and above all employers. From 1978 when the DES forced a new constitution on the doomed Schools' Council, there has been steady pressure towards lay participation in key decisions across the field of education. In particular, it is representatives of industry who have appeared in significant numbers on committees of all descriptions, whether they be concerned with national examinations, the teaching of English, governing bodies of all descriptions, the management of local pilot schemes such as those discussed above, or any other significant developments. Sometimes it seems unclear who remains in head-office to attend to the task of management!

The explicit purpose of such moves is to open up the claustrophobic world of education to the views of the consumer. But the implicit corollary must be that the influence of teachers and other professional educators should be diluted. Moreover, a further target appears to be the locally-elected politician who is no longer seen as a reliable representative of local opinion. As governing bodies are re-constituted under the 1986 Act to include much wider representation of parents, employers and other community representatives at the expense of the local authorities, the new Education Reform Bill will permit them to make

unilateral decisions to opt out of LEA control. Presumably such a decision would be based on avowedly educational reasoning and therefore
it will represent a judgement about curriculum, the way it is managed
and the way it is delivered.

Participation is, of course, not necessarily all it seems. The ludicrously
short period allowed for consultation on the various draft papers produced during the summer break of 1987 may well be seen as a sign that
it is essentially tokenistic. Moreover consultation, like experimentation,
is often no more than a device for defusing conflict: the views offered
are frequently self-cancelling, and the initial policy survives intact except
that a few practical pit-falls may have been averted. But, once again,
the significance lies not in the outcome but in the act. The state has
apparently made an honest attempt to accommodate the views of those
concerned, whether as individuals or as aggregated interest groups: having done so, its policies *and* its right to enforce them are rescued from
legitimation deficit.

* * *

Thus, there are very clear parallels between the strategies described by
Weiler and those adopted by the British Government in their attempts
to legitimize educational policy. But how long lived is legitimacy if the
policies do not survive on the ground? Can government intervention
retain credibility if, instead of appearing 'right and just', it is so undermined in practice that it soon appears to be ill-conceived and unfair?

In the situation thus being created, we must consider briefly the question of enforcement. There is a body of opinion which suggests that,
though central government may make prescriptions about a national
curriculum, the product as delivered, either through default or through
deliberate wrecking, may vary widely from what has been specified.
So far it seems that government is proposing to rely on the Inspectorate,
mandatory testing and the pressure of public opinion to ensure a
reasonable level of compliance. The role of the Inspectorate is far from
clear. At national level, HMI are presently few in number when
measured against the size of the task and the range of their other responsibilities. Even if quinquennial inspections were to become a reality,
they would scarcely seem adequate. On the other hand, LEA inspectors and advisers seem unlikely allies when the government is currently
undermining the position of the authorities who are their employers.

Can we believe they will ensure that the DES writ runs in schools which have 'opted out'? or in LEAs whose own curriculum policy initiatives are threatened? If an appreciable number of schools 'opt out', can we even assume that LEAs will any longer be able to maintain adequate support, including advisory services?

As yet there is no sign that the DES has devised sophisticated monitoring strategies such as those developed within TVEI. So we are back with testing and public opinion. Testing produces data, not solutions. To respond to the data requires time and resources for detailed follow-up and the link between test results and bringing defaulters into line is likely to be tenuous. Moreover, an effective response to unsatisfactory test results will necessarily pass discretion back to the professionals. Public opinion is equally problematic. Parents are far more diverse and inconsistent in their views than the Secretary of State would like to imagine. It is unlikely, for example, that he envisages the probability of litigation referred to earlier. Perhaps he would do well to pay attention to the view that unbridled parental choice is more likely to provoke local disputes about provision, rather than to create pressure towards compliance with the new curriculum. And it must not be forgotten that for many parents, over-sensitive to their child's apparent shortcomings, it will be hard to distinguish between failure on the part of the school to meet centrally prescribed requirements and failure on the part of the pupil to take advantage of the curriculum offered.

* * *

My argument therefore is that attempts to seek legitimation exclusively through the strategies identified by Weiler are inevitably going to be inadequate for, in themselves, processes of legalization, experimentation and an appeal to the public voice will not withstand failures at the implementation stage. Attempts at legitimation which do not recognize the need to carry professional opinion are foolhardy, to say the least. Experience of schemes such as TVEI may have encouraged government to think that despite initial uproar, a body of professional support sufficient to carry the day can be won over; but this is to ignore the fact that pilot schemes can often call upon a favourably-disposed constituency (Harland, 1987). The proposals in the current Education Reform Bill will affect every corner of the system, and will therefore need much broader acceptance than seems to be forthcoming at the present time.

Professional educators, on the other hand, cannot ignore the structural factors which constrain the state to address the management of the economy and the regulation of social life, both of which impinge upon the organization of education and training. Denying legitimacy to state action and state intervention may exacerbate the problem. If legitimation theory has any use for us, it may even be as simple as saying that whatever the state does, it must seek legitimation; and so, while it may be useful as a polemical device to attack it on these grounds, the denial of legitimacy cannot be substituted for an analysis of government policies. But for its part, on pragmatic grounds if not on grounds of principle, the state cannot afford to ignore the necessity to listen, and to act in such a way that it does not antagonize and alienate those from whom it needs support. And it is just on this point that the Government is manifestly failing. For example, last summer's consultative paper on the national curriculum (DES, 1987) is obviously the work of those whose certainties are firmly based on a lack of understanding of the nature of learning and teaching. Peter Cornall, the Senior County Inspector in Cornwall, describes the document (O'Connor, 1987, p.34) as 'paying only a dismissive lip-service to the professional enterprise and initiative on which all progress depends'. He goes on to speculate that the present shallow and hasty exercise compares but poorly with the fastidious and serious manner in which such matters are handled in France and Germany, countries with education systems which are apparently much closer to Conservative ideals than our own beleaguered edifice.[1]

* * *

In so far as the argument of this chapter leads to normative conclusions, the message would appear to be that increasing state intervention is to be explained by structural factors and it is these factors which account for the frenetic search for new forms of legitimation. Some but not all of those forms have been explored in these pages. What emerges is that opposition to the *fact* of intervention is not only likely

---

1. There is a longer extract from Cornall's speech in Clyde Chitty's chapter, pp.46-7.

to prove pointless but also will demonstrate a lack of understanding as to the *meaning* of such moves. However, it is equally apparent that unless government can convince us that their interventions are not only legitimate but also acceptable to professional opinion, then the chance that they will be subverted on the ground remains high. The most notable characteristic of countries which work successfully on the basis of a national curriculum is that, by and large, members of the teaching professions accept that this is how things should be.

References

Brighouse, T. (1987), letter in *The Independent,* 25 August.

Department of Education and Science (1987), *The National Curriculum 5-16: a consultation document,* London: HMSO, July.

Habermas, J. (1975), *Legitimation Crisis.* Boston: Beacon.

Harland, J. (1987), 'The TVEI experience; issues of control, response, and the professional role of teachers', in D. Gleeson, (ed.) *TVEI and Secondary Education: a critical appraisal.* Milton Keynes: Open University Press.

O'Connor, M. (1987), *Curriculum at the Crossroads:* an account of the SCDC national conference 'Aspects of Curriculum Change', University of Leeds, September 1987. London: School Curriculum Development Committee.

Weiler, H.N. (1983), 'West Germany: educational policy as compensatory legitimation', in R.M. Thomas, (ed.) *Politics and Education: cases from eleven nations.* Oxford: Pergamon.

Wilby, P. (1979), 'Habermas and the language of the modern state', *New Society,* 27 March.

Wuthnow, R. et al. (1984), *Cultural Analysis.* London: Routledge and Kegan Paul.

The National Curriculum and Special Educational Needs

Klaus Wedell

Over recent years, there have been significant advances in the principles and practice of education for those with special educational needs. The Warnock Report (DES, 1978) brought together much of the development of thinking up to that time, and the 1981 Education Act incorporated a considerable number of the recommendations emerging from it. Both the Warnock Report and the Act, which came into force in 1983, have led to a marked development of services to those with special educational needs, and to important changes in practice. The Educational Reform Bill of 1987 has to be evaluated in terms of these advances.

In this chapter, I plan to consider the Bill in relation to three of the main developments concerning the education of those with special educational needs:

1. The changed concept of special educational need;

2. The changes in educational practice and provision for those with special needs;

3. The recognition of the rights of those with special educational needs, and their parents.

The changed concept of special educational needs

The Warnock Committee affirmed that there was no basis for postulating a clear distinction between those who were handicapped and those who were not: 'It is . . . impossible to establish precise criteria for defining what constitutes handicap' (DES, 1978). In an educational context, the Warnock Committee recommended that a more relevant term was 'special educational need', a term first used by Gulliford (1970) as the title of a book. In the Committee's view, disabilities in a child called for compensating educational resources, and 'need' was used to refer both to the developmental, functional and other requirements resulting from a disability, and also to the requirement for relevant compensatory resources. In these senses, 'special educational needs' could be conceived as occurring in a continuum of degree, relative both to factors within the child and to the availability or otherwise of appropriate resources within the child's environment.

These concepts were clearly reflected in the definition of special educational needs stated at the beginning of the 1981 Act: 'a child has special educational needs if he has a learning difficulty which calls for special educational provision to be made for him'. This remarkable definition enshrines both the interactive nature of the causes which may lead to a child having difficulty in learning, and also unequivocally affirms the relativity of need. No indications are offered as to the criteria on which a 'call' for special educational provision might be based, but special educational provision is itself defined relatively as 'provision which is additional to, or otherwise different from, educational provision made generally . . . in schools maintained by the LEA'. The only further criterion offered is an operational one. In the case of those children whose needs are such that the LEA has to 'determine the special educational provision', the LEA has to maintain a 'Statement'. The Act thus recognizes two levels of need which are distinguished by the decision as to whether or not to implement this administrative procedure.

The Warnock Committee estimated that around 20 per cent of children might at some time in their schooling have special educational needs. This figure was based on prevalence studies such as those of Rutter et al. (1970). Since at that time approximately 2 per cent of children were in special schools or similar provision, it is evident that the majority of pupils with special educational needs were seen to be in ordinary schools. Department of Education and Science statistics for 1985 indicated that 18 per cent of LEAs had 1.3 per cent or fewer of their pupils with Statements, and 11 per cent had 2.1 per cent or more with Statements. This variability in percentages clearly reflects the difference in resources available within LEAs, and the point is further indicated by the fact that, in a recent research study, more metropolitan boroughs were found to have low statementing rates than shire counties (Wedell et al., 1987; Goacher et al. in press).

Unfortunately, there is no indication that the Education Reform Bill takes account of the 18 per cent or so of children with special educational needs in ordinary schools without Statements. The only reference to special educational needs occurs in Clause 10, which permits the national curriculum to be modified in the case of children with Statements. A similar paragraph (DES, 1987a, paragraph 40) occurs in the consultation document, which, however, suggests that pupils with Statements might be exempted from parts of the curriculum. Both formulations clearly have the paradoxical implication that, if a child moves from one LEA to another, its curricular requirements might also change. Quite apart from the educational principles raised by these points, it would seem that the current concepts of the nature of special educational needs incorporated in the 1981 Act, were not applied by the drafters of the Bill. However, since the drafting of the Bill, further thought seems to have been given to this issue. On 4 December 1987 the Government issued its response to the Report on Special Education of the Select Committee on Education (House of Commons, 1987) which states that the 'circumstances' which the Secretaries of State might define as appropriate to permit the modific ation of the statutory requirements of the curriculum, might include those children who had learning difficulties but who did not have Statements. This formulation was given in response to the Select Committee's expression of concern about the implication of the national curriculum requirements for pupils with special educational needs. It is difficult to know as yet, whether this change in the Government's position reflects a true recognition of the continuum of special educational need, and of the implications this might have for the delivery of the national curriculum not only for the 18 per cent of pupils about whom the Warnock Committee expressed concern, but also for the 40 per cent of pupils about whose education the previous Education Secretary was concerned.

Changes in education practice and provision
for those with special educational needs

The Warnock Committee, in its report, stated clearly that 'the purpose of education for all children is the same; the goals are the same. But the help that individual children need in progressing towards them will be different' (DES, 1978). This statement reflected the general recognition that, just as it was not possible, in an educational context, to draw a meaningful distinction between the 'handicapped' and the 'non-handicapped', so also one could not separate the education for those with special educational needs from education in general. Indeed, the general aims for education stated in the Warnock Report are not substantially incompatible with the aims stated in Clause 1, section 2 of the Bill. However, as the previous Senior Chief HMI, Sheila Browne, is reported to have said at the 1988 North of England Education Conference (*The Times Educational Supplement,* 8 January 1988), there is a considerable gap between these aims, and the core and foundation subjects in terms of which the national curriculum is described in Clause 3 of the Bill. This point was also made by a group of special educators in a memorandum setting out their response to the Government's consultation document:

> What appears to be missing from the discussions in the document is the breadth of curriculum objectives, in terms of personal and social accomplishments, as well as of subject achievements in conventional terms, which employers and parents now expect from education in both the independent and local authority sector. These accomplishments, which have national as well as individual importance and merit, cannot be nurtured unless the national curriculum is seen not merely as a set of subject study programmes, but as a basis for interaction between people and ideas (Fish et al., 1987).

These personal and social accomplishments have, of course, been given central importance in the education of those with special educational needs for many years. The role of ordinary schools in supporting pupils' development in these areas has become more evident in recent years, particularly with reference to the increasing awareness of the problems arising from pupils' disaffection and disruption. These aspects of the curriculum are also stressed in post-school programmes such as YTS. Indeed, the problems of youth unemployment have provided a clear example of the continuum of special educational needs associated with learning difficulty and personal growth and adjustment.

A very limited admission of the content areas omitted from the national curriculum is evident from paragraph 18 of the Government's consultation document. Health education and information technology are mentioned as 'themes' which are omitted from the proposed content

list. However, this is followed by the statement that 'such subjects or
themes should be taught through the foundation subjects, so that they
can be accommodated within the curriculum but without crowding out
the essential subjects'. Such a statement clearly implies that health
education is not regarded as essential and the implication contrasts with,
for example, the Government's acknowledgement of the overwhelm-
ing threat of AIDS.

It is evident from the foregoing that the content of the proposed
national curriculum does not match up to the aims stated. Consequently,
it not only fails the educational requirements of pupils in general, but,
by extension, fails to meet the requirements of those with special educational needs. Offering the latter the opportunity to have a modified
national curriculum might, if anything, be seen as singling them out
to have an opportunity to receive a curriculum which is more consonant with the Bill's general educational aims.

The 1981 Act requires governors 'to secure that the teachers in the
school are aware of the importance of identifying and providing for
those registered pupils who have special educational needs'. The Fish
Committee in its report (ILEA, 1985) made it clear that teachers could
meet this requirement only within the framework of the curriculum:

> Within its curriculum, a school has to decide on long and short-term goals;
> on sequences of progression, including progression in terms of concept
> formation and development; attitudes, ideas; knowledge and skills. The
> need for flexibility and for matching tasks to the individual implies that
> the sequence of goals in different curriculum areas may vary in respect
> of the needs of individuals and groups. It is very important for teachers
> to have a clear idea of progression in all aspects of the curriculum, and
> to use this for evaluating individual progress. It is on this basis for assess-
> ing the progress of all children, that it is possible to become aware of
> children who have special educational needs (para 2.7.6).

Both the Bill and the consultation document appear to promote a
form of assessment related to the curriculum. However, the formulations offered indicate confusion about the concepts of both content
and progression. The confusion about content is illustrated in the
example of health education given above. The consultation document
accords this some importance, but excludes it from explicit inclusion
in the curriculum, suggesting that it might constitute an emergent aspect
of foundation subjects. This of course, does not make health education

any less a part of curriculum content, and consequently one in which a pupil's progress should be monitored. The problem appears to lie in a confusion of the framework of the curriculum as relating to aspects of its delivery ('programmes of study' is a phrase used in the Bill) instead of content areas. (One can mentioned in passing, that this confusion also shows that insufficient account was taken of the effect which failure explicitly to list a relevant curriculum content area has on the importance ascribed to it.) Clearly, in the context of the requirement for teachers to identify pupils' special educational needs as demanded by the 1981 Education Act, the omission of key areas of the curriculum would have serious consequences.

The same risk unfortunately may also follow from the confusion about another aspect of the framework of the curriculum in the consultation document and the Bill. Progression is mentioned in the quotation from the Fish Report as another essential dimension of the curriculum framework. The following point is made in the memorandum of special educators referred to above:

> There appears to be a confusion in the consultation document about the questions being asked. For example, in order to monitor the standards achieved by a class, school or an LEA, it is necessary to obtain, among other information, data on norm-referenced attainment levels, which might be based on the *sequence* of a national curriculum. However, planning the progress of an individual or group of pupils is based on the *progression* of learning steps within the curriculum, and on the teacher's ability to apply this to the process of the pupil's learning (Fish et al., 1987).

This quotation indicates the way in which the Bill and the consultation document fail to distinguish between the so-called 'stages of assessment' and curricular progression. It is obvious that these are not unrelated, but there is confusion about how they should be applied to identifying and meeting pupils' special educational needs in the framework of the curriculum as it is envisaged in the Fish Report, and in the 1981 Act. Once again it has to be pointed out that the confusion does not only affect those with special educational needs. A group of special educators have stated in a briefing paper:

> for all pupils, whether or not they have special educational needs, there is a next step in the progression of their learning, the achievement of

which requires continuous rather than periodic assessment . . . For pupils with special educational needs, just as for unusually able pupils, the next step may not be level with an age-appropriate norm, but the teacher's commitment in both instances is to help the pupil achieve his or her next step. The pupil's effort in learning and the teachers in teaching has to be assessed in terms of the effective progress through these steps, if they are to be accorded their due credit (Wedell et al., 1988).

It is interesting to note that the above considerations seem, in general, to have been taken into account by the Task Group on Assessment and Testing in its report (DES, 1987c). Its recommendatiions stress that the assessment of the individual pupil's learning should be carried out in relation to curricular progression and content. Furthermore, the Task Group recognizes that its assessment procedures have to be formulated in terms of the national curriculum as propounded by the curriculum working parties. (In passing, one might mention that this point illustrates the illogicality of setting up separate agencies for assessment and curriculum development.)

It is possible that the problem arising from the confusion about the nature and purposes of assessment as put forward in the consultation document and the Bill may, to some extent, be averted if the suggestions of the Task Group on Assessment and Testing are implemented. To this extent, schools and their staff may be enabled to meet the requirements of the 1981 Act, and so some of the fears expressed about the implications of the national curriculum by the Select Committee in its report in Special Education (House of Commons, 1987) might be allayed. However, there is no doubt that both identifying and meeting the special educational needs of pupils present formidable professional challenges to teachers in schools, and require backing from support staff and in-service training. Research on the implementation of the 1981 Act shows that many LEAs are committed to increasing the number of pupils whose special educational needs they are intending to meet in ordinary schools. Data also indicate that more staff are being directed to supporting teachers in ordinary schools (Wedell et al., 1987; Goacher et al., in press). It remains to be seen how these trends will continue in the current context of constrained resources and also in the wake of the implementation of an Act following the Bill. Some concerns about this, however, arise already from the proposed provisions of the Bill itself, and will be considered in the following section.

The recognition of the rights of those with special educational needs and their parents

I shall confine consideration of this sub-topic to the issue of integration and to the rights of parents to take part in decisions about the education of children who have special educational needs.

The 1981 Act states that children with special educational needs should, as far as practicable, be educated in ordinary schools. The question therefore arises as to whether the Bill will facilitate schools' capacity to meet the pupils' special educational needs. The provisions of the Bill are explicitly intended to increase parental choice, and, to this extent, the aims of the Bill are consonant with the 1981 Act's promotion of parental participation in the decisions about their children's education. Unfortunately, however, the Bill seems more likely to reduce the support available to pupils with special educational needs, and so reduce the range of choice of schools for the parents of such children. Three aspects of the Bill seem to indicate this possible trend.

Firstly, the Secretary of State is quoted in a DES press release (DES, 1987b) as saying 'The Bill will introduce competition into the public provision of education'. Those concerned for the education of pupils with special educational needs cannot be reassured by the provisions of the Bill, that one of the criteria for competition will be the quality of schools' support for these pupils. It has already been stated above that there is only one mention of special educational needs in the Bill (apart from a reference to Special Schools.) This seems particularly strange since Schedule 10 makes it clear that the Bill is seen to require only two minor administrative amendments to the 1981 Act.

Considerable concern has been expressed in memoranda sent to the DES by special educators in response to the consultation document, that the proposed publication of pupils' achievement levels would force teachers to reduce their commitments to pupils with special educational needs. Moreover, the Bill's clauses on financial delegation, and on the proposals for schools to opt out or to change their nature, make no explicit provision that the quality of a school's support for pupils with special educational needs should be considered in these decisions.

The Task Group on Assessment and Testing were, according to their report, aware of the dangers which might follow from inappropriate use of assessment data. The briefing paper on the Act, which was mentioned above, states:

Staff of schools are likely to direct their efforts away from pupils with special educational needs, if the assessment of pupils' attainments at the four stages is used for the wrong purposes. Clear guidance on the collection of this information and on the use of the data derived will need to be given to the schools, the LEAs and all those with relevant responsibility, to ensure that a school's resource potential for pupils with special educational needs is not put in jeopardy, but, rather, is enhanced (Wedell et al., 1988).

The briefing paper goes on to point out that, if schools fail to make adequate provision, a deluge of demands will follow for pupils to be given Statements, so that support can be secured for them. However, even this cannot be described as a means for ensuring parental choice, in the light of research findings (Wedell et al., 1987; Goacher et al., in press).

Secondly, the procedure by which it is proposed that decisions should be made about schools opting out not only fails to ensure consideration of support for pupils with special educational needs, but also leaves the parents of these children vulnerable with regard to the voting procedures. By definition, such parents will always be in a minority, and, by definition, they themselves will have little influence in a vote, particularly since it is proposed that decisions should be made on a simple numerical majority of those voting. Even assuming that the parents of other children might value the educational consequences for all pupils which can follow from the integration of pupils with special educational needs, the impact of the problems associated with the points I am making is likely to influence their final decision.

Thirdly, support for pupils with special educational needs in the ordinary school is currently made on an LEA-wide basis. However the Bill does not mention how this will be carried over when schools opt out, and colleges become independent. Clause 75, for example, requires LEAs to 'treat pupils at grant-maintained schools no less favourably than at schools maintained by them'. However, the very fluid administrative situation which will occur if schools opt out, change their nature, and possibly opt in again, will greatly exacerbate the problems which already exist for responsible LEA staff in planning and maintaining provision. Although the Government, in its response to the Select Committee report, stated that Circular 3/74 on the allocation of staffing for pupils with special educational needs would be revised, it is well known that the change to integrated provision has made this a very difficult brief to fulfil. Furthermore, it is far from clear how the requirements of such a Circular could be implemented. Problems would arise, for example, with the allocation of staff employed by the LEA, with staff shared between opted out and non-opted out schools, with staff employed wholly within a single school, with staff acting as part of a special school's outreach programme, and with staff working on 'bridging courses' between schools and colleges.

It seems clear that the integration of pupils with special educational needs would certainly not be made easier by the implementation of the Bill in its present form. Furthermore, parents choosing schools for their children with special educational needs would be faced with considerably greater uncertainty than they already experience at present.

Conclusion

The proposals of the Education Reform Bill might, according to the Secretary of State, be summarized in three words, 'standards, freedom and choice'. Each of these words has relevance for the education of pupils with special educational needs and their parents, just as much as for all pupils and their parents. Furthermore, Mr. Baker has affirmed that the Government's purpose is 'A better education — relevant to the late twentieth century and beyond — for all our children, whatever their ability, wherever they live, whatever type of school their parents choose for them' (DES, 1987b). Those concerned for the education of children with special educational needs would share these aspirations without reservation. However, our examination of the provisions contained in the Bill raises many doubts as to whether the aims will be achieved by the means proposed. It is evident that a few significant alterations have already been made in the nature of the Bill's proposals. The recently-published report of the Task Group on Assessment and Testing also indicates a recognition of some discrepancies between the Bill's aims and the means to achieve them. However, at least as far as pupils with special educational needs are concerned, there is still a very long way to go. For these pupils and their parents, the passing of the 1981 Act represented the beginning of a statutory commitment to meeting their needs which the Education Reform Bill as presented to Parliament has done nothing to confirm.

References

Department of Education and Science (1978), *Special Educational Needs* (Warnock Report). London: HMSO.

—— (1987a), *The National Curriculum 5-16: a consultation document.* London: DES, July.

—— (1987b), Press Release 343/87, 'The Education Reform Bill', 20 November.

—— (1987c), *National Curriculum: Task Group on Assessment and Testing: a report.* London: DES, December.

Fish, J., Mongon, D., Evans, P. and Wedell, K. (1987), 'Memorandum to the Department of Education and Science in response to the consultation document on the national curriculum'. London: Institute of Education, University of London, Library Archive Collection 199/1987-88.

Goacher, B., Evans, J., Welton, J. and Wedell, K. (in press), *Policy and Provision for Special Educational Needs.* London: Cassell.

Gulliford, R. (1970), *Special Educational Needs.* London: Routledge and Kegan Paul.

House of Commons (1987), *Special Educational Needs: implementation of the Education Act 1981:* Third Report from the Education, Science and Arts Committee, Session 1986-87. Together with Proceedings of the Committee, Minutes of Evidence and Appendices. London: HMSO, 2 vols.

Inner London Education Authority (1985), *Equal Opportunities for All?* (Fish Report). London: ILEA.

Rutter, M., Tizard, J. and Whitmore, K. (1970), *Education, Health and Behaviour.* Harlow: Longman.

Wedell, K., Evans, J., Goacher, B. and Welton, J. (1987), 'The 1981 Education Act: policy and provision for special educational needs', *Special Education,* Vol.14, No.2, pp.50-3.

Wedell, K. et al. (1988), 'The Education Reform Bill and provision for children and young people with special educational needs'. London: Institute of Education, University of London, Library Archive Collection 199/1987-88.

An Unconstitutional National Curriculum

John White

It's amazing how wrong one can be. It is nearly twenty years since I first began arguing for a national curriculum. In all that time, I have been assuming that once the need for such a curriculum had been established and people began to think about its more determinate shape, they would be embarking on a pretty complex task. They would have to work out a coherent and defensible set of overall aims, examine what sub-aims, or intermediate aims, these might generate on logical, psychological and other grounds, bear in mind the wide variety of ways by which aims might be realized, try to work out criteria delimiting the role of central government from that of local government, governing bodies and schools . . . All this would be a long and massive undertaking, requiring the collaboration of professionals, civil servants, politicians and others in some kind of semi-independent but politically-accountable National Educational Council.

I now feel a complete idiot. As the Government's proposals show, devising a national curriculum is simplicity itself. You pick ten foundation subjects to fill 80-90 per cent of the school timetable, highlight three as of particular importance and arrange for tests at different ages. I could have worked out the national curriculum years ago. Anyone could.

* * *

But perhaps things are more complicated than this. There must be some reason, surely, why the Secretaries of State picked out their ten foundation subjects and their three core subjects as particularly important. There must be underlying ends to which they see these as means. What could they be?

Clues in the national curriculum consultation document itself are not easy to come by. Rationale is not in general its strong suit: it gives every impression of having been written by people used to issuing orders with no questions asked. Perhaps with hundred-plus majorities in prospect until the end of the century, reason-giving as a political practice has itself come to seem to some less than rational. Whatever the explanation, the justifications given for this choice of curriculum subjects are extremely attenuated.

In paragraph 16, we read:

> But the foundation subjects commonly take up 80 per cent of the curriculum in schools where there is good practice. The Secretaries of State will take that as their starting point . . .

This does not get us very far. If good practice can be identified, of course it is a good idea to use it as a starting-point. But how do you identify good practice? And what criteria, more particularly, are the Secretaries of State using to pick this out? We are not told.

Is there enlightenment elsewhere? In earlier sections of the document there are scattered references to generally agreed aims of education. In paragraph 4, for instance, we read about

> policies for the school curriculum which will develop the potential of all pupils and equip them for the responsibilities of citizenship and for the challenge of employment in tomorrow's world.

This is not the most intellectually satisfying account of the aims of education that one might hope for, and it is perhaps a shade on the brief side. Most people will agree that education should have something to do with personal development, with citizenship and with employment, but disagreements of all kinds begin to break out once one tries to say something more substantive. What is needed is not a bland list of headings like these, but a more fully-worked-out set of aims, with reasons for giving them the particular substance that they have. Again, it is clearly not enough to spell out the content of each aim in independence from others: interrelations and priorities among them must also be made fully explicit. (How is personal development related to citizenship, for instance? Are these discrete, and possibly conflicting, aims? Or is preparation for citizenship a *part* of promoting personal development?)

The passage just quoted, for all its brevity, is the longest account in the document of the aims which are to underpin the national curriculum. Reference is also made, it is true, to aims set out in the 1985 White Paper, *Better Schools*. This provided a longer list of headings than the one just given; but it is still only a list and is open to the objections about lack of substance, lack of rationale and lack of any indication of priorities spelt out in the last paragraph.

Still, in these reason-sparse times we must make do with what we can find. How do the aims provided, either in the national curriculum document or in *Better Schools,* map on to the ten foundation and three core subjects? Presumably English, maths, science, a modern foreign language, technology, history and so on are included because they are seen as promoting personal development, citizenship, vocational aims and so on. But *how,* exactly? Are they all equally important vehicles for each aim? Or are some subjects more conducive to some things than to others? Is music as relevant to citizenship aims (supposing some determinate content is given to these) as history?

No doubt some kind of reasonable justificatory story could be told to ground these subjects in these aims. Whatever else it would be, it would be long and complex. But the document provides no hint of what it might be. It also has another lacuna. An adequate rationale must not only show how subjects are conducive to aims, but also give reasons why these subjects have been chosen in preference to other ways by which aims might be realized. There are two demands embedded here. First, why *these* subjects? Why, for instance, are Latin and sociology excluded? (I am not necessarily advocating these.) Secondly, why *subjects?* Don't the Secretaries of State know that schools and teachers seek to realize their aims in all sorts of ways — sometimes via subjects, sometimes via forms of activity in which subject boundaries are deliberately crossed, sometimes via instantiation in pedagogy, sometimes via school ethos and organization . . . the list could go on and on. There is only one point in the document at which its thinking goes momentarily beyond a subject framework. In paragraph 18 it acknowledges 'subjects or themes such as health education and the use of information technology'. But it quickly makes it plain that 'such subjects or themes should be taught through the foundation subjects'. The wayward horse is soon reined in.

No reason is given why the foundation subjects are to be the vehicle for aims. Take the Government's citizenship aim again. No doubt the foundation subjects can be useful here in all sorts of ways. But so can other subjects; sociology for instance, or economics. And so can things which transcend a subject framework altogether, like community studies, a whole school anti-racist policy, a school organized as a participatory democracy, teaching methods premised on equality of respect for all participants. If the Secretaries of State had taken the broader view, had seen that national curriculum planning must begin with aims and then work outwards into their manifold realizations, they would not have been left with this intellectually impoverished jumble of disconnected ideas hyperbolized as the 'national curriculum'.

The logical gaps in its argument at point after point are glaring and distressing. I feel sure the Secretaries of State could have done more to close them. Mr. Baker, after all, is an intellectual. He tells the nation that he is one on television programmes, alluding to the Glorious Revolution or to the South Sea Bubble with all the infectiousness of a would-be A.J.P. Taylor. How can he — an Oxford man as well — have allowed his name to be put to such a shoddy product? 'We must raise standards consistently', he tells us in paragraph 6. Agreed. But why did he not start in his own office?

If Mr. Baker's background in history failed to give him a sufficient training in logical thinking, why did he not exploit the talents of the three philosophers publicly known to be sympathetic to his cause? (There may be one or two covert admirers, it is true; and three is not to be sneezed at, representing as it does a now not insignificant and indeed ever-increasing proportion of the sum-total of academic philosophers, so decimated by this Government.) Anthony Flew, Roger Scruton and Oliver Letwin are all perfectly competent to monitor logical defects of this order of grossness. They can do it rather well. The trouble must be that they spend so much of their time looking for reds under BEds and in other places that the energy they can spare to shield their own side's documents from public disgrace must be very limited.

*   *   *

We know that Mark Carlisle and Sir Keith Joseph devoted the full power of their minds over many years to laying the foundation for the national curriculum — to warming the oven and kneading the dough, one is tempted to say, for the master baker to come. How chagrined they must be to see their efforts crowned by the soggy sponge cake of a national curriculum that now emerges!

But perhaps I am not doing justice to Mr. Baker and his predecessors. It is easy to point to the intellectual shortcomings of the document — to its inattentiveness to underlying aims and so on — but that would be unfair and irrelevant if the defects were shown to be in some way excusable. Perhaps the Secretaries of State were over-preoccupied by their party's election promises to act quickly on a national curriculum, seeing action rather than reflection as the immediate priority? If they were, I suggest that they will regret their precipitateness, if they have not done so already. Even now (as I write) they have been forced to backtrack on the percentages of timetable time for different subjects. Perhaps by the time this book is published other foundations of the new structure will have been abanonded, perhaps the foundation, or core, subjects, or perhaps even the subject-based framework itself. It is hard to see all this resting intact under the critical barrage which it has already undergone and may be expected to suffer in the next few months.

Whether the explanation of the shortcomings is immoderate haste, I do not know. The only piece of evidence I have in favour is anecdotal. Some time in the late spring of 1987, a week or so before the General Election was called, an acquaintance from another institution rang me to invite me to a meeting with one of Mr. Baker's aides. 'The Secretary of State wants to know how to go about introducing a national curriculum. Can you come to a meeting with us next Tuesday morning?' This chance to change the face of English history I declined with the utmost reluctance, making some reference — unless my memory is playing tricks — to having to take my daughter's pet weasel to be spayed that morning.

The incident shows two things: first, a certain lack of practical nous in calling on one who privately thinks of himself as the Hammer of the Right to help them out of a jam; and secondly, and more germanely, that as late as last May the Secretary of State had not the slightest clue about how to set up a national curriculum. It all points to a rush job, from first to last.

*   *   *

There is another, quite different, explanation for the lack of rationale in the national curriculum document. This is that the Tories know, consciously or unconsciously, that they cannot publicly justify the political policy underlying the curriculum proposals. Like other parties, they want to raise pupils' academic attainments, especialy in areas like English, maths and science, which are held to be helpful to economic growth. *Unlike* other parties, they want to do this in such a way that pupils do not become critical of the society in which they live, disposed to question authority in all its forms, not least in the workplace. This is the only obvious way of making sense of their elevation of economy-related 'core' subjects, and their squeezing out of social and political studies by ensuring that virtually all the timetable is spent on other things.

This is a difficult path for the Tories to tread, as I shall be suggesting below, but it is a quite impossible line to justify publicly. For what it entails is that pupils at state schools are to be viewed, by and large, only as means to the furtherance of economic aims: if the economy wants a better trained workforce, the schools will provide it. If pupils *were* being treated as ends in themselves, their need to understand, criticize and have some say in shaping the institutions and communities in which they live and work would not have been brushed aside. What government could openly admit that it saw pupils as only of instrumental value, only as means to others' ends? Those parents prepared to back the Tories in their talk of raising standards for their children might well be the first to be alienated once these illiberal implications were made explicit.

The basic anti-humaneness of this policy is obscured to some extent by the widespread belief that personal well-being consists in occupying one of the more dominant positions in the social pecking-order, with all the advantages in money, leisure, power and recognition which commonly attend them. Those who end up towards the top of the pile, aided by a successful scholastic career, may feel that their schooling has indeed been directed towards their own good and that they have been far from treated in a purely instrumental way. It is doubtful whether they are right. Power, money and status can be the prerequisities of conformists, of gilded slaves. The only sure indication that pupils are not being treated as tools is that they are actively encouraged to take responsibility for their own lives, to do what they do out of some personal conviction that it is right and good, and not simply because authority or custom tell them to.

This obscurity about the nature of personal well-being has helped the Tories, I suggest, to persuade a large number of parents — both those whose children do in fact 'make it' and those who at least have aspirations in this direction — that the sort of economy-orientated curriculum here envisaged is in their children's interests and so to be applauded. There are enough parents in these categories — especially in the second — to make the Tory championing of parent power a political winner and to make it reasonable to assume that, despite all the teaching profession's carpings about the national curriculum, it will command broad popular support.

Once it is made clearer, however, that for the great majority of children and perhaps, as has been hinted, even for future supervisors and managers, this is not a curriculum for personal empowerment but for subservience to capital's and bureaucracy's demands; and once it is made clearer that human well-being can consist of far more than the possession of power, wealth and status; the Tories' recipe may come to look less inviting. *This* is why they have traditionally been chary of giving full justifications of their policies on education; when everything is spelt out, the inconsistencies between their sales-pitch and their underlying motivations become too glaring.

Present-day capitalism's legitimation crisis in education will not be lessened, but, I suggest, exacerbated by these proposals for a national curriculum. Whether it is through the improvement of schooling since the war or through the liberating effects of television and other media I do not know, but the extent to which people in this country now want to lead their own lives and no longer be beholden to or pushed around by authority is an undeniable feature of our way of life. (Even Marks and Spencer has difficulty these days in training up a biddable sales-force.) The national curriculum can be plausibly seen as a crude attempt to put the lid on the growing taste for personal autonomy among the masses (products of independent schools, who are *not* to be constrained by national curriculum, are seen as quite another matter). But the water in the pot is boiling too fast. Authoritarian solutions will no longer work. Even with their impregnable parliamentary majority, Conservatives will have to show more finesse than this in their attempts at social control.

* * *

Deeper questions remain about political obligation. There is no virtue in a national curriculum as such. Hitler had a national curriculum, and so did Stalin. The basic issue is: what *kind* of national curriculum is Mr. Baker giving us?[1]

I take it that the question whether there should be a national curriculum at all is now behind us. The *theoretical* case for shifting from professional to political control is unanswerable. What curricula schools should have takes us directly into the question as to what kind of society we should be living in. This is a central — *the* central — political question: in a democracy teachers have no special rights vis-à-vis the whole citizenry in helping to decide this. There is every reason why the broad aims should be nationally determined, with further guidelines blocked in at LEA level. At the same time schools should be maximally free to work out how these political prescriptions are to be implemented: at this level teachers *do* have the professional expertise to determine what should be done.

But not just any national curriculum will do. If we rule out totalitarian versions, on what principles do we do so? We take for granted, surely, that we wish to live in a free, democratic country in which ordinary people are not the puppets of those in government and have each an equal right to participate in political decision-making. A nationa' curriculum should reflect this social ideal of personal and political self-determination.

In what way? It could do so in a weaker or in a stronger sense. It could at least do nothing to erode these kinds of autonomy as we enjoy them now; or it could actively foster them. There are many ways in which political action in general could improve things here. On the personal side, many obstacles still block the autonomous way of life as a universal ideal: for many people poverty, ignorance, prejudice, preventable illness, unemployment, or authoritarian working conditions oblige them to make do with lives not of their own choosing. Politically, ignorance again, inequalities in power and influence between the ordinary voter and, say, the newspaper magnate or trades union boss, the absence of proportional representation, the limited scope for workplace democracy — all these make it harder for us collectively to determine our social life.

The main test of the constitutionality of a national curriculum is

---

1. This question is also looked at in other contributions, notably in Clyde Chitty's paper.

whether it helps to promote personal and political self-determination. Other branches of government besides education must tackle some of the problems raised above — poverty and unemployment, for instance. What education can do is to enlarge the forms of understanding and cultivate the dispositions of mind and character required for these forms of autonomy. Pupils will need to acquire a broad understanding of: different ways of life which they could choose, including different occupations; obstacles to their pursuing preferred ways of life and means of overcoming them; the nature of democracy and its underlying values; the particular political arrangements of their own society and the main political issues which it faces; world politics. Among the dispositions they will need are: critical attitudes towards authority, moral courage, self-confidence, practical judgement, the desire to protect and promote the self-determination of others.

There is no evidence that the national curriculum meets these criteria. In particular, it excludes the whole area of political education and the understanding of one's own and other societies on which this rests. There is nothing in its list of subjects or its reference to national tests to suggest that these would be out of place in a totalitarian regime.

Schools and LEAs would have good reason, therefore, not to comply with these prescriptions without better evidence of their benign intentions. If we take them together with other government policies, they look anything but benign. The main thrust of recent initiatives has been towards stratification within the educational system to subserve what are seen as the differentiated needs of the economy. Personal and political autonomy have been nowhere on the agenda.

The big question mark over Mr. Baker's curriculum is whether it is not an indoctrinatory instrument. We should not be diverted by Tory charges that state schools are riddled with indoctrination on the part of peace educators and others. Indoctrination is basically to do with preventing reflection. Directly inculcating doctrines is only one way of doing this (and there is precious little evidence that this is what peace educators are up to). A most powerful way of indoctrinating pupils is by so organizing their studies that certain kinds of reflection — about political matters, for instance — are off the agenda. This was not possible for governments to achieve directly before the recent shift from professional control of curricula; but now, by filling school timetables with safe subjects, by determining much of the syllabuses to be covered, and by focusing teachers' attention on getting pupils through national tests, preventing thought about fundamental values is a much more feasible task. We need to see through the rhetoric of the national curriculum. The idea is rightly popular in the abstract, since it can seem to help every child to get the same worthwhile education. But those parents who support this version of it might find themselves buying not liberation for their children, but imprisonment. The illiberal features of Mr. Baker's proposals must now be brought home to them. Blur or disguise the issues as he is bound to do, his critics' pressure on him to square his curriculum with the basic values of our constitution is now not going to let up.

FORUM

for the discussion of new trends in education

FORUM, founded in 1958, is an independent journal addressed to progressive classroom teachers, heads and administrators, as well as to parents interested in understanding more about new developments and trends in education.

FORUM is run by teachers: the editorial board is drawn from infant, junior and comprehensive schools, adult and community education, administration and teacher education. It is an entirely independent journal, having no connection with any established organization or institution.

FORUM keeps close to the classroom, but it is also alive to the issues behind the news and behind new developments in education. It has been in the forefront of the move towards comprehensive education and towards mixed ability grouping in primary and secondary schools — trends which FORUM pioneered.

Articles regularly discuss the content and methods of education: new teaching methods, classroom organization, curriculum, multicultural education, assessment, profiles, classroom and school management. Government policy is regularly analysed and assessed.

Publication dates: September, January, May.

Subscription to FORUM (£5.00 p.a.) to:
The Business Manager, FORUM, 7 Bollington Road,
Oadby, Leicester, LE2 4ND

BEDFORD WAY PAPERS

educational studies and related areas

THE GCSE: AN UNCOMMON EXAMINATION (BWP 29)

Caroline Gipps (ed.)

The establishment of the General Certificate of Secondary Education (GCSE) has been described as one of the most significant educational innovations of the past half century. The authors of this Bedford Way Paper set out the background to the introduction of the new examination and discuss the issues and problems to which it gives rise.

Among major issues discussed are the question of whether the aim of a common examination at 16-plus will be subverted through the presence of differentiated papers and questions; the problems associated with including course work within the assessment; questions posed by the extension of assessment by teachers; whether it will be possible successfully to employ grade criteria; and the role of and thinking behind GCSE within the total context of assessment at secondary level. Concerns highlighted include whether the new examination will lead to an enhanced professional role for teachers and whether it will succeed in the end in permitting a greater range of pupil ability to be assessed.

The volume is published in the belief that a full debate of the issue of assessment and its relationship to the curriculum and pedagogy of the secondary school is all important at this fledgling stage of the new examination.

BEDFORD WAY PAPERS
educational studies and related areas

EDUCATION FOR A PLURALIST SOCIETY (BWP 30)

Graham Haydon (ed.)

The Swann Report, *Education for All* (published in 1985), presents the response of an official inquiry to a profoundly important question as we move towards the last decade of the present century: how should education respond to the diversity of culture, faith and ethnic background which characterizes present-day British society?

The chapters collected in this volume are by philosophers of education who, from the perspective of their discipline, attempt to explore further some of the reflections and conclusions of the Swann Report. Two of the contributors discuss what the 'framework of commonly accepted values' for which the report calls might consist of, and how it might be arrived at; another probes more deeply into the notion of prejudice; another looks at the question of racism and self-esteem among pupils; two others contend that there is more to be said than Swann recognizes for separate religious schools of a certain kind within the maintained system, and for positive discrimination in the appointment of ethnic minority teachers.

Given the complexity and importance of the subject it is not surprising that the contributors fail to agree with one another on all points. But there is a common recognition that the school and teachers have a crucial role to play in any movement towards a genuinely pluralist society. The volume should be seen as a contribution to a debate of momentous import; each of its chapters sketches a possibility or a line of argument that demands to be taken seriously.

BEDFORD WAY PAPERS

educational studies and related areas

LESSONS IN PARTNERSHIP (BWP31)

E. Cowne and B. Norwich (eds.)

Early in 1983, the Department of Education and Science announced the introduction of centrally funded, one-term, in-service courses for teachers in what were designated as priority areas. This Bedford Way Paper is concerned with the experience of one of these courses (given the acronym OTIS), on meeting special educational needs in ordinary schools, provided at the University of London Institute of Education. The main emphasis of the course has been on the needs of individual schools and for its success it has depended on the close involvement of local education authority officers and headteachers.

After three years of co-ordinating nine OTIS courses, the authors, both course tutors, here set out to describe and evaluate what has been for them 'a novel and challenging venture'. As befits the collaborative nature of the course, the viewpoints of LEA advisers, headteachers, and the teacher course members themselves, are included. There is a full analysis of the genesis and development of the course, and descriptions of the effect it has had in schools. In a final chapter the authors reflect on what the various participants have learned from the experience and on general in-service educational (INSET) issues.

Lessons in Partnership will be of interest to anyone involved in or concerned about the development of INSET, whether LEA, school, or college-based, whether focused on the needs of the school or of the individual teacher. The publication is especially timely in view of the introduction of new funding arrangements which, given adequate resources, will open up new and exciting possibilities of further INSET provision on the collaborative pattern here described.

BEDFORD WAY PAPERS

educational studies and related areas

REDEFINING THE COMPREHENSIVE EXPERIENCE (BWP 32)

Clyde Chitty (ed.)

The 'comprehensive revolution' was launched some twenty years ago with a variety of objectives, including the provision of a school system that would be both more efficient and just in developing the abilities of *all* pupils. Today, more than 90 per cent of British pupils attend secondary schools of a non-selective nature. Yet public confidence in the comprehensive system is being undermined. The present Education Secretary regards it as 'seriously flawed' and, along with other educational issues, it was a key point of discussion in the 1987 general election campaign. A Conservative Government has been returned determined to introduce radical changes. What future remains for the comprehensive experience?

The contributors to this Bedford Way Paper are all committed to a belief in this experience — though it needs to be redefined in terms of the current situation and needs. In far too many cases achievement within an academic curriculum stemming from the grammar school has been the only kind which counted. But the 'new vocationalism' is being introduced in a manner that could bring a similar narrowing of education and exclusion. The volume argues for a curriculum that synthesizes the academic and the vocational and protects a broad educational experience for all, and for a variety of organizational forms within the comprehensive framework. That framework remains the best hope for all the nation's children.